Melanie Dale is funny, which is a trait th[...] person. But, even more than that, she's aut[...] to say the things we all think, but wonder if [...] loud. And that's exactly what she does in *It's Not Fair*. As she shares her own stories, you will laugh hard, nod your head, and feel like maybe she's looking right into your heart. You won't regret the time you spend reading her words and will walk away relieved that someone understands exactly how you feel.

Melanie Shankle, *New York Times* bestselling author of *Nobody's Cuter Than You*

I love this book. Melanie has the rare gift of being able to encourage you through our hardest days while making you laugh until tears stream down your cheeks.

Alli Worthington, author of *Breaking Busy: How to Find Peace and Purpose in a World of Crazy*

It's great to have friends who cheer you on when life is shiny and happy and Pinterest-y, but it's invaluable — critical, even — to have friends who cheer you on, empathize, and encourage when life takes a turn and looks nothing like you imagined. Fortunately for all of us, Melanie Dale is that friend. She's hilarious, wise, and boasts an uncanny ability to relate *Doctor Who* to any situation (it's one of the lesser known spiritual gifts). In *It's Not Fair*, Melanie is at her very best because (1) she's a crazy-gifted writer and (2) *she gets it*. Whatever your "it" is, you'll walk away from this book (which is *delightful* to read) feeling like you've found a new friend, and as an added bonus, you'll also feel like you've found some new perspective that just so happens to be grounded in and covered with Truth. Melanie's fancy like that.

Sophie Hudson, author of *Giddy Up, Eunice* and *Home Is Where My People Are*

Melanie never fails to make me laugh, and in *It's Not Fair* she turns her hilarity to one of life's hardest subjects: suffering. Sharing her own stories of disappointment and challenge, she offers no easy answers but leads us on a path to hope, stopping for laughter along the way. She is the friend you want beside you when life gets hard.

Sandra Stanley, North Point Ministries

Melanie Dale is the most hilarious, real, non-cheerleader, Bible-believing, movie-quoting cheerleader you would want to stumble into during your life's toughest struggles. She doesn't try to give you the perfect answer or ten tips to take away your pain — she simply reminds you that you aren't alone. She shares her own junk through hilarious tales and sometimes tear-jerking tales and inspires us all to take one step to love the life we didn't choose.

Courtney DeFeo, creator of Lil Light O' Mine
and author of *In This House, We Will Giggle*

The best time for comic relief? When you're going through a trial, of course! And only Melanie Dale, with her quick wit and big heart, can weave both hilarity and compassion into those hard seasons of life we all know in some form. *It's Not Fair* is a funny, entertaining, and highly relevant read. Whatever your circumstances are, this book will remind you that laughter is medicine to the soul and hardships are always more bearable when you have a friend who understands.

Kari Kampakis, blogger and author of *Liked: Whose Approval Are You Living For?* and *10 Ultimate Truths Girls Should Know*

Melanie Dale is as good as it gets. She's a wise, tiny Buddha trapped in a comedic shell; the fearless, oh-so hilarious girlfriend we all wish we had. Luckily, we get to keep her on our nightstand now. (In the not creepy way.)

Erin Loechner, writer & stylist

Understood. That's exactly how I felt while reading *It's Not Fair*. Finally there's a voice with the courage to talk about the tough reality of what it's like when your dream doesn't come true, or the tough reality that happens after your dream comes true and isn't what you thought it would be. Not only does Melanie dare to speak the truth, she does it in a way that keeps us laughing and going deeper in faith at the same time. So grateful for this read!

Jamie C. Martin, author of *Give Your Child the World: Raising Globally Minded Kids One Book at a Time*

Here's the thing, life isn't fair. Our parents said it, we've said it to our own kids, and we've thought it plenty of times too. But when Melanie Dale says it, she's not blanketing hardship in a statement that "fixes it" without really fixing it at all. In her "me too" relatability, readers find in Melanie a sister, a friend, and a delightful guide to find the beauty in the hardship, the gifts in the midst of pain, and even fulfillment in the longing. I'll read Melanie Dale till the cows come home because I know that this gal is as real as they come and in her words I find not only camaraderie, but more importantly, I find Jesus.

Logan Wolfram, author of *Curious Faith: Rediscovering Hope in the God of Possibility*, speaker, and Mel's real life friend

With a writing style that's both side-splitting funny and heart-healing real, Melanie Dale is an author whose life-giving words stay with you like those of your most trusted friend. Her writing matches her personality: sparkling and engaging. Read Melanie's words and be encouraged in every way possible.

Kristen Strong, author of *Girl Meets Change: Truths to Carry You through Life's Transitions*

If you ever wonder, "am I the only one who...?" or "does anyone understand...?" then grab this book and you'll discover you are not alone and you'll find a true friend who's funny and honest and who will encourage you.

Susan Alexander Yates, author of many books
including the new *Risky Faith: Becoming Brave Enough
to Trust the God Who Is Bigger Than Your World*

Laughter isn't a typical response to suffering, but Melanie shows us why laughter is not only one of the acceptable — but essential — ways to cope with the unfair and unexpected potholes in life. Even better, she reacquaints us with a God who not only welcomes our anger about our suffering but a God who remains ever present and faithful in it.

Melanie's wicked sense of humor makes this a must read for anyone who needs a refreshing take on the familiar topic of suffering. I absolutely loved this book.

Jeannie Cunnion, author of *Parenting the Wholehearted Child*

First of all, Melanie Dale had me at her "menstrual cramps emoji." I think we've all been waiting for years for that to be developed. Second, she's just so real, and funny, and warm, in a "here's me sitting next to you" way. Life can be fun, joyful, and buoyant — it can also be a real mess. When we feel disappointed, angry, and like shredding something with our bare hands, Melanie gets it, and she points us in the most winsome ways to the One who also sits next to us, getting us, holding us, and healing us.

Lorilee Craker, bestselling author of thirteen books,
including *Money Secrets of the Amish* and *Anne
of Green Gables, My Daughter and Me*.

It's Not Fair

LEARNING TO LOVE THE LIFE
YOU DIDN'T CHOOSE

Melanie Dale

ZONDERVAN

It's Not Fair
Copyright © 2016 by Melanie Dale

Requests for information should be addressed to:
Zondervan, 3900 Sparks Dr. SE, Grand Rapids, Michigan 49546

ISBN 978-0-310-34216-8 (ebook)

Library of Congress Cataloging-in-Publication Data

Names: Dale, Melanie, author.
Title: It's not fair : learning to love the life you didn't choose / Melanie Dale.
Description: Grand Rapids : Zondervan, 2016.
Identifiers: LCCN 2016010860 | ISBN 9780310342144 (softcover)
Subjects: LCSH: Christian women--Religious life. | Expectation (Psychology)--
    Religious aspects--Christianity. | Christian life.
Classification: LCC BV4527 .D245 2016 | DDC 248.8/6--dc23 LC record available at
    https://lccn.loc.gov/2016010860

Cover design: James Hall
Cover photo: © Paper Boat Creative / Getty Images®
Interior design: Kait Lamphere
Interior illustrations: Melanie Dale

First printing June 2016

For Elliott, Evelyn, and Anastasia.
I love our life together.

Contents

-PART-
ONE

The Part of the Book Where I Explain the Book a Lot

Skipping this part could induce dire consequences, like that time you missed the first class, didn't get the syllabus, spent the entire semester confused, and got an F. And this book is about life. You don't want an F in life, do you? I wouldn't risk it.

PART ONE

The Part of the Book Where I Explain the Book a Lot

A Help-Each-Other Book

> Buttercup: You mock my pain.
>
> Man in Black: Life is pain, Highness. Anyone who says differently is selling something.
>
> —*The Princess Bride*[1]

So you've just found out some hard news. He's cheating. She's cheating. The thingy isn't benign. Your child got a diagnosis. You didn't get the job. You were demoted. You didn't get the job and the person who has made your professional life a living hell did get the job.

Or maybe you've been living in this state of suspended misery for a while now. It's like you're hanging from the ceiling looking down on your life on fire, wondering how you got here and how to put out the flames.

Sometimes when life falls apart and then on top of that your basement floods and your dog dies, the only acceptable response is hysterical laughter. When things get so far gone, so spectacularly a world away from any plans you made or dreams you dreamed, you feel it bubbling up inside of you, and you scream, "It's not fair!" And it isn't. Fair is an illusion and life is weird.

So what do you do? You have all these things piling on, and you don't know how much more you can carry before the bag breaks and everything drops all over the ground and rolls across the parking lot. You didn't choose these things; you weren't prepared. If you'd known what was coming, you would've done more cardio or taken more vitamins, maybe hidden money under the mattress or run screaming out of the building. This wasn't the plan. And it's bad and it's hard and you're tired.

It's not fair.

I'm sorry. I really am.

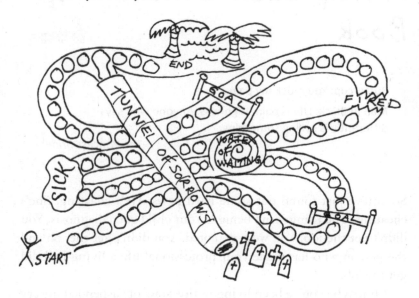

I want this book to be the friend you put in your bag and take to the hospital. It's for when you're passed over for the promotion or when he doesn't propose or when he leaves. You won't find any easy answers or a 12-step plan here.

I wish we were meeting for coffee and talking in person so I could listen to your story. In good friendships, that's what we do, right? We listen to each other and respond with empathy and encouragement. This book is me trying to do that through pages. But since I can't hear you, this is kind of one-sided and I'm over here sharing from my perspective based on my own stuff. But your stuff is important too. In fact, your stuff is the reason I'm trying to gather my thoughts and write them down.

It's a sometimes sucky journey, but you're not alone.

Dragging My Mess Next to Yours

I can't solve your stuff. I wish I could, but it's your stuff and your journey through it. This isn't really a self-help book. I hope it's helpful but not in a "here's what you do" way. More in a "here's me sitting next to you" way. A help-each-other book.

If I'm not careful, I can be ridiculously depressing. Who wants to hear about someone else's shattering disappointments when we're all up to our eyebrows in our own? Or worse, my life will seem like kindergarten to you. Like the preschool of pain, when you're deep into a PhD dissertation on "The Absolute Worst Thing That Anyone Has Ever Dealt With." If so, I apologize in advance for my whining and how irritating it might sound.

I'm going to mix together some of my own hard things, some junk that helps me, crappy drawings, and probably a little bit of inspiring stuff. And movie quotes, duh.

I have a confession. I thought I was done with the hard part and was going to impart to you how you, too, could get through pain and come out on the other side. But that's a lie. In the middle of waxing on about fairness, my life sort of fell apart again. Apparently we don't learn to love our lives and then check a box when it's done. We learn to love our lives every day, one day at a time, forever. So hi, from within the trench. It kinda smells down here. I wish neither of us were here. But I'm glad we have each other.

Your story won't look the same as mine. There is no formula for dealing with suffering. I won't insult you with a one-size-fits-most mentality about the pain. All I'm going to do is drag my mess next to yours and invite you to drag yours next to mine.

We relate to one another through our stories, don't we? I love a good story, one with hope, or people falling down but getting back up, or people falling down because they slipped on a banana peel. I love a good poop story or a funny movie quote. And when I'm desperate and feel alone in the world, I love a friend who will just spend time, share life, and talk about the thing without trying to solve everything. So I'm going to introduce you to some of my friends who have agreed to share their stories here. We need all the help we can get from each other.

About Me

I should probably tell you a little about myself. I've been married to my college sweet-heart, Alex, for fifteen years. I met him as a prospective student at Denison University, where he was playing guitar in the campus coffee shop, The Bandersnatch, in an acoustic duo. He has no recollection of this momentous occasion, which makes me feel super. Just like the movies. Months later when he noticed my existence, we didn't like each other. At all. There might have been glaring. And that's how the magic really happened.

Over time, we discovered our mutual love of the color orange and our total commitment to performing entire conversations by quoting movies. I converted him to Whedonism, the illustrious fandom devoted to all things Joss Whedon, the creator of *Buffy the Vampire Slayer*, and he introduced me to the sardonic humor of Chevy Chase. We bonded over sarcasm and Christian retreats involving singing around campfires and sharing our favorite Bible verses and much making out. Maybe not all that at the same time.

We've pretty much grown up together, at least the whole adult part of our lives, and somehow in spite of everything we've weathered together, we're still hard-core in love. I think the movie couple that best represents us is, well, I want to say Iron Man and Pepper Potts, except with Alex as Pepper and me as Iron Man, because Alex is really good at business and running things and keeping me in line and I'm really good at flying all over and shooting bad guys with my thrusters.

Anyway, over the course of a twelve-year marathon filled with

Via Facebook @UnexpectedMel

The kids just discovered my bike lock combination.

Elliott: Mommy, it's T-U-R-D.

Ana: Toord? Waht ees toord?

Elliott: No, it's turd. Turd!

Evie: Turd. Turd.

Yay for learning how to read . . .

needles and paper cuts, we have accrued three children. Our first, Elliott, who just this second turned eight, was born after a five-year battle with infertility. My body tried to kill him and we barely made it to the third trimester together, thanks preeclampsia, but after a cozy little NICU stay in a baby tanning bed for him and lots of drugs for me, we both made it out of the hospital alive and mostly fine-ish. We brought Miss Evie home from Ethiopia when she was almost two, after lots of trials and misfires for us and especially for her. And then last year, when she was nine, Ana Banana decided to join us from Latvia. My kids could write a better book about unfairness and learning to love the lives they definitely didn't choose. (I hope someday they do and cast Tina Fey to play me in the movie version.)

I've spent bajillions of hours trying to figure out how to talk about my kids. Where do my stories end and theirs begin? How do I tell you enough about our family life so you can find common ground without over-exposing them? For better or worse, Mommy is an author and blogger. I tell myself at least we don't have a reality show.

I've listened to adult adoptees and friends who grew up in the foster system. I've talked with a friend who's the daughter of an author. I've asked my whole tribe to pray for wisdom, talked to other authors, and consulted my editor.

So after much prayer and advice, here's what I will say: within our family, we are dealing with autism, mental illness, ADHD, and trauma. Honestly? All the things I worried about before I became a mom, all the things we secretly fear deep down and maybe don't even say out loud, have happened in our family.

"Just don't let it be____."

"As long as it isn't____."

And yet. Every day I learn a bit more to love this life I didn't choose. And now that I'm here, I wonder why I was so scared. I wish I could take away all the pain from my kids, but as their mom, I wouldn't trade their precious personalities for anything. As our family therapist says, "'Normal' is just a setting on the dryer."

Much of what I'd tell you about my kids if I took you on a tour of our home life isn't really mine to tell. I have to look these children in the eye and know that I've left their stories to them. And so all I'll say is my three, quirky kiddos each walk their own special roads, and when combined, these roads make one heck of a city map. It's jumbled and difficult to navigate for all of us, and we deal with traffic and gnarls daily. But our city is bustling and full of energy and sometimes I walk these streets and marvel at the life they contain. For this book, there's a whole lot of unfairnesses that I can't reveal. So I'll stick to the ones I can.

For those of you living with people on their own special roads . . . solidarity. We are learning to love these lives none of us has chosen. Our city lights burn brightly.

I love my family and we are fun and funny people. The five of us are all unique and special and every day we combine our quirks into a family and practice loving each other well. I say practice because, as you probably know, families take a lot of practice and a lot of work, whether it's the family you live with now or the one you grew up with.

That's us in a nutshell. You'll hear lots more details later in a mishy-mashy way, sometimes out of chronological order. If you confuse Evie with Ana, or wonder when I had that operation I was talking about, or why I'm *still* talking about infertility after there are clearly kids all up in here, don't worry. I can't keep my life straight either. Think of my ponderings as a season of *Doctor Who*, very timey-whimey, but I will endeavor to avoid a paradox that could irrevocably destroy the space-time continuum.

Via Twitter @UnexpectedMel

My daughters are trying to teach my son how to burp on command. We like to destroy gender stereotypes around here. And also, apparently, we're gross.

Laugh to Keep from Crying

"You have to laugh to keep from crying," my mom has always said, and I've embraced that. But crying is great too, and sometimes we cry while laughing, which is probably the world's most perfect feeling. And so I've always done a lot of Emotion Blending, like a cry-laugh smoothie that comes out my nose and works all the facial muscles.

My editor told me to put in some disclaimers. Please be advised:

If you are struggling with clinical depression, anything life-threatening at all, anything that needs doctors or people with lots of degrees by their names, or medicine, or anything official, by all means go get the party pack of all of that. We have a whole team with an array of letters and diplomas surrounding our family right now. Professionals are really important. I am not that. And if at any point you experience discomfort lasting longer than four hours, please seek medical attention immediately. Additional side effects may include meat sweats, bacne, helmet hair, spirit fingers, front butt, fungal toe, spontaneous rectal combustion, Hobbit feet, whooping snort laugh, man hands, zombie breath, increased cravings for squirt cheese, fear of Pottery Barn, auctioneer voice, raisin boobs, and excessive hyperbole.

Did I forget anything? If I'm ever too weird, inappropriate, dumb, or off-putting, then by all means feel free to download all ten seasons of *Friends* instead, and thank you for your time.

Sometimes I'm a little overdramatic.

My dad, on the other hand, *is* really, really calm and steady. It's one of the many reasons I don't think biology has much to do with family because HOW COULD WE SHARE DNA?!? I mean, really. Despite our differences in temperament, I adore this man. And growing up, he was my rock. Whenever I'd get kerfloofy over one or six of the many things I had swirling around at all times, he'd grab some quality time with me, listen, ask lots of questions, and usually, at some point during my diatribe, he'd start laughing. Gently laughing. I mean, I was sixteen, so I'd still get huffy about it, but now as a grown-up, I so appreciate this approach to the hard stuff, and I laugh with myself all the time. Sometimes I laugh *at* myself, but mostly when things are hard, I laugh *with* myself, gently, just like my dad taught me to do.

In Genesis when the Lord told infertile old Sarah she'd get pregnant, she laughed. Sarah laughed in the midst of her pain when she encountered a message that seemed ludicrous (Genesis 18:12). That so resonates with me. Laughter as a coping mechanism for pain. And then Abraham named the baby Isaac, which means "he laughs." The whole nation of Israel was launched with laughter (Genesis 21:3).

How do you write a book about learning to love your life in the midst of suffering? Madeleine L'Engle said, "The only way to cope with something deadly serious is to try to treat it a little lightly."[2] Yes, there will be days when you just can't. There've been whole weeks during my low points when a smile felt like a stretch. But just in case . . . let's keep the option open to grin through our tears.

Mary's Story: Marines and Maggots

While battling my first bout of non-Hodgkin's lymphoma, my treatment was like rafting down an unknown river. As a Long Island gal, Billy Joel's "River of Dreams" seemed to be the sound track of my life during that time.

Despite the hair loss, chemo, and keeping an Excel spreadsheet of my kids' schedules and sleepovers with friends and relatives, the lunacy of it all did not escape me. As I rode the rapids toward my bone marrow transplant, I could not get over the sheer comedy that comes from trying to live a typical life in such an atypical way. Morbid humor is truly something that must be embedded in one's DNA, because it can seem really inappropriate at times. Not to mention, people really don't know how to react or treat you when, well you know, you have no eyelashes, eyebrows, head hair, and just look like a freak.

In my case, nearly 100 percent of the time, most people, when totally surprised or unguarded, responded with kindness and genuine compassion. This was most evident in two cases. My neighbor Jim, a sixty-five-year-old former Marine from the Greatest Generation, opened the door to find me in my gray hoodie, sloppy warm-up pants, scruffy sneakers, red bandana covering my cue ball head of no hair, red eyes from crying out of frustration, and a face mask. I had just waved good-bye to my children, who were being parceled out to loving friends for a few weeks as I prepared to go to Johns Hopkins for my transplant (twelve-week stay).

Unfortunately I was locked out of my house. When Jim opened the door, his face went into shock. Without a word, his face clearly said, "I am being mugged in broad daylight by a druggie gang member!" Once I saw that he didn't recognize me—why not?—I quickly said, "Hi, Jim, it's me, Mary, from across the street, and I am locked out. Can you help me?" His demeanor changed in a nanosecond. Without skipping a heartbeat he said, "Oh, Mary, [cough, gulp], I am so sorry. I didn't recognize you there. Must be these glasses [as he wiped them]." His graceful save made me smile, as did his breaking-and-entering skills using a credit card.

Not one week later, as I lay in my hospital bed, I felt another ripple of gallows humor. The female doctor, clearly practicing her bedside manner, sat on my bed, leaned in to tell me how my treatment was progressing, and the whole time had an angelic look and a purposeful calming cadence to her voice. All were useless. Once seated, I looked at her navy blue mono-grammed name that was embroidered on her crisp white doctor's coat—Dr. Maggot. Whatever she said, I couldn't hear, as my insides were busting and I was trying ever so gallantly not to cry from laughter or pee my pants (bedpan optional). It made me wonder about so many things, most notably how a person with the name Maggot would go into medicine. When she asked if I had any questions, I fought the urge to spit out, "Have you ever thought of using an umlaut with your name?"

From that point forward, I knew that funny, illogical, and nonsensical stuff happens every day and will continue to be there even when you are thrust into a gushing river of unfair stuff. You just need to keep looking for it and finding it.

—*Mary W.*

You Might Hate This Book

Maybe you'll need to throw this book against a wall and tell me I'm an idiot and don't understand life. I wouldn't even mind that, because it would be a sign you're reading it.

And I'm not a theologian, so what could I possibly say about God at a time like this in your life? If you aren't sure how you feel about God, you're safe with me. I mean, I hope you feel safe with me. I would leave God out of this whole discussion, except I don't know how. If you're kind of side-eyed about the whole thing, I get it. Feel free to lump the Bible verses in with the movie lines, just words I like to quote. They're much more than that for me, but they don't have to be for you.

By now you may have guessed that I am unqualified to pontificate about what makes life fair or unfair and that I am an unreliable narrator in exploring how to deal with life's hard things.

I have a BFA in theater, so I think that makes me licensed to instruct you on the proper use of jazz hands and how to speak iambic pentameter. I am the quirky friend you call for a pep talk or to agree with you that your boyfriend is a total bunghole and you are so better than that. I can try to cheer you up by stuffing one hundred M&Ms in my mouth at one time (I have done this for realsies). I can't make your situation any better, but maybe I can make your heart a little lighter. Maybe.

I'll sit by you and hold your hand and bring you French-pressed Ethiopian coffee and Rainbow Nerds, two of life's most precious offerings. Alex says I need to tell you what else I can give you, like wisdom and quantifiable takeaways. Charts! Maps! S.M.A.R.T. Goals! This book will solve all of your problems!

I'm not everyone's cup of dark roast coffee. I know that. So, if you find yourself wanting to scream at me and tell me how I stink and how I don't understand and where to stick this stupid book, go right ahead.

Wait. Let me assume tornado-drill position and cover my head with my interlocked fingers. Okay, now go ahead.

We Make Each Other Better Humans

When you're going through something difficult, sometimes you tend to cut yourself off from others because no one understands, or people say stupid things, or you don't have the energy to perform up to the standards that society expects. (What do you mean we have to shower multiple times a week?!? This is crazy talk.)

But we need each other. We don't need hordes of people, but we need a few to tether us to reality and remind us why our altered life might still be worth living.

I've come to the conclusion that relationships are the most important things in life. We were created for relationships with each other and with God. We make each other better humans.

It isn't easy letting others into our lives, especially when we're messy and cracked. It takes vulnerability, like slipping off your hospital gown to show the doctor where it hurts. We brave the cold exam table and open ourselves up to scrutiny.

And we receive healing. Friends help us feel not hopeless. They receive our freak-outs and mental breakdowns and deliver hot coffee and cold compresses.

We need to remind each other that we're not alone, to see that other people have survived difficult things and lived to smile another day, to know that even as we're broken and horribly mangled, we're still worth loving and we aren't abandoned. We need to tell each other these things. We're survivors, and we need to survive together and we need each other to survive. So let's write a help-each-other book together, okay?

-PART-

TWO

All the Feels

*For When You Need Something
More Than an Emoji*

MALESTROM

JAZZ HANDS

MENSTRUAL CRAMPS

FACE PALM

BARFING ALIEN

F-BOMB

I Feel Your Pain

Brick Tamland: I read somewhere their periods attract bears.
Bears can smell the menstruation.

Brian Fantana: Well, that's just great. You hear that, Ed? Bears.
Now you're putting the whole station in jeopardy.

—*Anchorman*[1]

I'm not really into politics. Arguing makes me sweaty, and politics seems like a lot of arguing. It's one of those things I know is probably super important, but I'd rather live my life knowing it's out there being important but not directly interacting with it in my actual life, like the space program or *Dancing with the Stars*.

While I don't really get into politics, I do love *Saturday Night Live*'s impressions of politicians and in fact, I sometimes get so wrapped up in the funny fake versions that I think they're the real people. I mean, I think we're all a little unsure about Sarah Palin and Tina Fey and which one can see Russia from her house and which one wrote *Bossypants* . . . or wait, is that the same person?

Anyway, I'll never forget Darrell Hammond's Bill Clinton, with his adorable lip biting and "I feel your pain." I can't remember if President Clinton actually felt people's pain or if it was just *SNL*'s version of the pain feeling, but real or pretend, it's forever stuck in my mind.

So in this chunk of the book, I feel your pain. I am full-on, lip-biting, thumbs-upping feeling your pain over here.

Even when we haven't gone through the same thing, we can dig into our own stuff and find empathy. We can say, "I can't understand what you're going through, but I'm with you, and I know you're hurting, and I'm sorry."

We can share the pain and confusion of not understanding why things happen the way they do.

There's heart pain, and then there's body pain, and I've had both, and maybe you have too. I've had endometriosis for as long as I've had a working uterus, I think. It's a fun little disease because nobody knows much about it, even the smart people, and some people go their whole lives with it and have no problems, and some of us have chronic pain and infertility—the whole works.

Life Is Painful. Period.

Dear Handful of Men reading this book,
*   I'm about to talk about my period. You've been warned.*
Woman up and read on. You can do this.

Love and tampons,
Melanie

I realized I might have a problem the first time I got my period. I was at Girl Scout camp, away from home for a week, and I was living in nature. I am a devout indoor girl, but I'd found a camp called "Twilight Zone," where you stay up all night and sleep all day. It sounded perfect, so I went for it, even though I'd be cramming into one week my allotted outside time for the year.

We were on a hike, and I got my period and began barfing in the bushes as we walked. Those Girl Scouts are no joke, because we kept hiking, pausing for me to barf every few seconds. Maybe this is why I hate hiking to this day.

I'd read the Judy Blume books. I'd gone to the seminars where teen girls talked about their monthly friends like this was a big important coming-of-age story for women. But my entire body was coming inside out and I thought I might die on the trail like the settlers from that Oregon Trail computer game we used to play in the eighties. I wanted to yell, "Save yourselves! Roll me into the ditch and go!"

Blinding pain. And it came back every month. Like a phone bill. Like a phone bill that punched you in the gut so hard it made stuff come out both ends. Picture the worst muscle cramp you've ever gotten. Now center it in your lower abdomen. Add radiating pain and throbbing throughout your entire torso. Plus shooting pain down your legs. And the time you threw your lower back out and couldn't stand up straight and cried like a wee little baby. Add in that too.

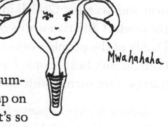

Mwahahaha

One time in the greenroom for a summer musical, I had a man tell me, "Strap on a maxi pad and deal with it." Aw, that's so precious. What an adorable precious baby person he is. I'm short, but I can do an unnerving stare, and I may have threatened him with bodily harm. In college I knew Alex was The One when he made me a Belgian waffle and brought it to my dorm and stroked my hair while I did Lamaze breathing and moaned.

Heavy Narcotics and a Pelvic Exam

About eleven years ago, the endo kicked it up a notch and decided monthly pain wasn't enough. Chronic daily pain became the new norm, with my right ovary feeling skewered like a human kabob. It was so dramatically different that I went to the hospital thinking I had appendicitis, where I experienced two firsts: heavy narcotics and a pelvic exam by a male doctor. Thankfully, the narcotics came first. By the time Doctor Dude came in the room, I was so loopy Ronald Reagan could've performed the exam.

Not appendicitis. Probably endometriosis. Now we knew, and knowing's half the battle. Well, not really. Knowing is one-sixteenth of the battle . . . maybe. Okay, actually in my case, knowing did jack squatty.

I underwent laparoscopy to diagnose and fix it, and as the anesthesia began to wear off, I felt the familiar knife through my ovary and my heart sunk. Still there.

It's still there now as I write these words. I've learned to live with it, and it's probably part of the reason why I love sitting so much.

Sitting is the best.

In 2 Corinthians 12:7–10, Paul talked about praying for God to remove some kind of ailment or issue that he had. He prayed over and over, but God didn't heal him. Even though he was, like, the model Christian who was telling everyone about Jesus, the Big Daddy of the people working it for God. Which reminds me that God doesn't heal people based on merit or what we're doing for him or if we earn it with extreme Christianness.

Because of these surpassingly great revelations . . . to keep me from becoming conceited, I was given a thorn in my flesh, a messenger of Satan, to torment me. Three times I pleaded with the Lord to take it away from me. But he said to me, "My grace is sufficient for you, for my power is made perfect in weakness." Therefore I will boast all the more gladly about my weaknesses, so that Christ's power may rest on me. That is why, for Christ's sake, I delight in weaknesses, in insults, in hardships, in persecutions, in difficulties. For when I am weak, then I am strong.

Via Twitter @UnexpectedMel
Dear endometriosis,
Go fluff yourself.
  Love,
  Melanie

Whatever Paul had, it sounds rough. Maybe he had cramps too. Maybe I'll start calling mine "messenger of Satan."

If you're suffering from chronic pain, or temporary pain, or heart pain, or head pain, I feel your pain. I feel it in my stupid ovary. And I'm sorry. We are mighty warriors. We are intrepid. Ain't nobody gonna bring us down.

Note: As I'm writing this, my ovary has decided to go berserk, like it heard me typing about it. It knows all, sees all. Creepy li'l guy. I've had a couple of ultrasounds and am trying to decide what to do about it. *Shhh.* Don't tell him I'm talking about him, or he might light himself on fire and take out my whole torso.

Additional note: I'm not sure why my personified right ovary is male.

Amy's Story: Pushing Through the Pain

I don't get out of the house very much because the strain of getting all the kids packed into the car and out the door can cause problems. It is rather difficult to drive well when you are having trouble sitting up straight in the driver's seat. So when my health is weaker, we stay home. When my health is stronger, I go and do as much as I can before my health fails again. Some days the pain is difficult. Other days I am so exhausted, I don't want to move.

But God gives me just enough endurance and strength for that day. Not always an abundance. Most days I feel like I have been drained of every ounce of energy I have and my body is throbbing from head to toe by the time I fall into bed, but God has been there with me each step of the way. There is always enough. God is teaching me to depend more on him. When I am well, I tend to feel like I can do it all myself, and my pride gets in the way. God does what he needs to do for me to teach me to lean on him.

My health probably won't get better. In fact, it will probably get worse. This life can be lonely, isolating, painful, discouraging, and draining. I get angry at times because I miss my old life. I miss going hiking with my husband. I miss being able to wander around stores for hours with my girlfriends. I choose to trust that God is good. I will keep choosing to trust God each day for the ounces of energy that I need for that day.

—Amy T.

Finding Out If Dad Is Dead

A few years ago, I thought my dad was dead for about an hour. One afternoon, my mom called and said, "Melanie, they're taking him to the hospital . . . they won't let me see him." She had arrived home to find EMTs over my dad with paddles doing the whole "Clear!" thing. Apparently he recognized that he was having a heart attack, called 911, then collapsed.

I asked Alex to watch the kids and took off to my parents' house. On the way over, I started crying, but then stopped to talk out loud to God, because I process everything with words. I told him, "It's too soon. I'm not ready. But God, he really loves you, so if he's with you now, then I know he's really happy. But I thought we'd have more time."

It's weird thinking back now to that conversation with God. I was torn between this utter desolation at the thought of not having my dad and this odd peace that he got what he's always wanted, to be with Jesus. This is the man I've seen spend every morning with his Bible and highlighter. He's had this steady faith, no real mountains or valleys, just a steady discipline of pursuing a relationship with God. It's the same relational steadiness he's exhibited in his relationship with my mom, my brother, and me. He just shows up. Every day. Small increments of mundane time units. And over the course of a life, he has this healthy legacy of faith and family that's a constant reminder to me that our faith works. Somehow it works. So if he was dead, I knew he was right where he wanted to be. It was as if he was in the car with me reminding me, as he had so often, that God is sovereign and on the throne.

I had an out-of-body experience at that point in the car ride. Like "Huh. So this is my reaction to my dad's death. I can't

Via Twitter @UnexpectedMel

Evie found a roly poly and "loved" it to death.

Me: Sweetie, I think he's dead.

Evie: It's okay if he's dead. I still love him.

imagine the next few weeks and months and years, and oh, what about all the memories, and how do I tell Elliott . . . but huh. My first reaction is that I know where he is and who he's with." I don't think I fully realized how my faith worked until that moment.

It was March Madness, a season for our family that comes with no small amount of excitement and fervor filled with a whole lot of Kentucky Wildcats. I flashed back a couple of weeks earlier when Dad had invited my brother and me to a sports bar to eat wings and drink a beer and watch a game. (I feel like my dad would want you to know that he's not a beer drinker. He's more of a cabernet sauvignon kind of guy. And I'm not a sporty person. But in this very real actual story of us, there was both beer and sports. Go figure.) The three of us stayed out till 1:00 a.m., cheering for the Cats in a bar in Georgia, where exactly zero other people cared. Thinking my dad now was dead, I was so glad we'd had that beer, we'd eaten those wings, we'd stayed out past our bedtimes on a school night.

When I arrived, the EMTs were loading up and I walked in the house to find my mom, who freaks out over everything (Hot brakes fail! Slippery when wet! Bridges freeze before roads!)—except when a ginormous crisis occurs, and she thinks she's lost her best friend, the friend she's known since they were twelve. Apparently when Ginormous Crises occur, her type-A planning capabilities override her need to panic and I found her in the kitchen calmly packing a bag of snacks and water bottles because we'd probably get hungry at the hospital. She apologized for bothering me and said she just needed me to drop her off at the hospital and then I could get back home to the kids. I told her I'd probably stick around for a while, you know, just to see if Daddy was dead and oh, I dunno, maybe keep her company.

We got to the hospital, and she again encouraged me to get home to my life. I let her know that this was my life and I was staying. I offered to contact her friends and she *pshawed* me and told me not to bother them. I bothered them anyway. Because that's what good friends are for, for bothering in times of crisis.

Mom and I sat calmly in the waiting room of the cath lab, as if we were waiting for mani pedis and not To Find Out If Dad Is Dead.

He was not dead.

We were very relieved.

The nurses came out to update us, and apparently many factors aligned perfectly to save his life. It was—literally—no really, literally—unbelievable. He'd had a heart attack in what they call The Widowmaker part of the heart. Very low chance of survival. It happened to be his day off, so he was home. My parents happen to live fairly close to the hospital. He happened to call 911 before he collapsed because he happened to have had a small incident years before and recognized the signs. The hospital happened to have opened a new cath lab and had a system equipped to handle this as quickly as it did.

Via Twitter @UnexpectedMel

Elliott: God, thank you for friends, because if we didn't have friends, it would be no good.

The EMT who saved his life came to his room in the ICU and started crying, because he'd never seen someone live through what had happened. Daddy's heart doctor stopped by and kept asking him questions to try to figure out how he could still be alive. It didn't make any sense to anyone.

I got to see him after they put in the stent that saved his life, and as they wheeled him toward recovery, they paused for Mom and me to see him. I told him Elliott said to feel better, and his eyes filled with tears that ran down his temples on each side into his hair. Later in ICU he said God still had work for him to do and immediately started naming the relationships he was forming and the conversations he was having with people. Not his veterinary work, although that's important to him. Not service hours in the community, although he does that with a generous heart. No, he talked about still being around for the relationships.

At this point, if you've lost someone, and here I am talking about not losing someone, feel free to throw the book. I'll ask the Zonderpeeps if we can make these things with extra sturdy bindings for repeated throwing. It's not fair. So completely not fair.

At the same time my dad was not dead, we found out that someone else in our family-in-law was dead, way before his time. Too soon. So incredibly too soon. We told Daddy in his ICU bed what had happened, and he wished he could trade places. He wished and wished that he could trade places with the young daddy who still had so much living to do. I have tears in my eyes right now just remembering it.

Life doesn't make sense.

When miracles happen, all I know to do is to be grateful. I don't understand why sometimes we get the miraculous and sometimes we get the devastating. I don't know why God allows this or that to happen. It's not fair.

Audrey's Story: No Matter What Bad Things Happen

I am twelve years old, have dark brown hair, and a big scar from my lungs down to my pelvis. I had ovarian germ cell cancer. I know someone who has my cancer, and he has had more than eighty surgeries. I only had six. I don't think it is fair that so many kids die of cancer and I didn't, but then again I don't want to be dead.

I have been to nine funerals in the past four years, and that's just the people I know. People would always come up to me and say how proud of me they were about how hard I fought while I was in treatment, but there are still kids who died who fought just as hard as me, but they didn't make it.

Hope works in many ways. Hope can be when you are holding on to that little piece of life that you don't want to let go. Hope is also when you don't have any life to hold on to, but you just think maybe a miracle could happen.

I have hope because I believe in God and that this life we are living now is only the beginnings to our real life in heaven. No matter what bad things happen on earth, it can't affect what happens to us in heaven.

Hope is strange and mysterious, but you should never give up no matter what the circumstances are. That hope is what I held on to during my cancer treatments.

—Audrey A.

At the End of Yourself

If things get bad enough, and your hope starts to dribble away, sometimes your brain can start to do wonky things. Mine did. Deep into the Infertile Wasteland, when I'd been on a cycle of needles and disappointment for more months and years than I could count, my reason jumped the shark, and I headed down a one-way road to badness.

Lying on the couch in pain, a human lab rat who was running out of places to poke, I started thinking more and more about loving Alex and the life I wanted for him. I thought about how I was holding him back from becoming an amazing father, and I thought about the medicine cabinet filled with pills from all my hospital visits. Maybe the greatest gift I could give him was getting out of the way. I hit bottom.

Full House. Click.
7th Heaven. Click.
Some show with tween Olson twins. Click.
Clifford the Big Red Dog. Click.

I lay on the couch, curtains drawn, day after day, watching hours of television, trying to stay numb. If people rang the doorbell, I ignored them and hid. I kept a heating pad on my abdomen and called the doctor when I ran out of pills to help the pain.

We stayed active in church, especially in our couples' group where everyone was always pregnant, and I threw baby showers and knitted blankets. I went to work, helped start a theater company, wrote reams of scripts that no one ever saw.

DC was a transient town for a twenty-something, and my growing despair went unnoticed by most. I hid.

But as I went in and out of hospitals and doctors' offices, and my medicine cabinet filled with prescriptions for the pain in my ovary, I began to wonder if the pills would help the pain in my heart.

It would take only a few short steps, just a few short steps and a few seconds to the bathroom, to the cabinet, to the pills that could free Alex forever from my infertility. He could find a fertile wife and have the life he always wanted raising kids. And maybe New Wife would iron.

I was at the end of myself, when your brain starts making wonky connections and playing out twisted scenarios and it's like you're trapped inside one of those Salvador Dali paintings with the melty clocks. I was a melty clock draped off the side of a table. And I seriously thought maybe killing myself was the selfless thing to do. That's some kind of abstract art.

> **Via Twitter @UnexpectedMel**
>
> *Me: I'm so nervous I'm going to miss something in my book edits.*
>
> *Alex: As long as you don't have "your" instead of "you're."*
>
> *Me: Now I have nightmares. Thanks for that.*

If your circumstances have your brain playing out those scenarios, please take this book with you to the waiting room at the counselor's office. Keep reading, but read there while you wait for someone who can help. I've been there, but I'm just me, and all I have is empathy and The Electric Slide.

Depression is a sly little devil. I didn't realize I was depressed at the time. I actually thought I was a little sad but really handling things okay as I watched *Full House* marathons all day and contemplated ending it for the good of my husband's sperm. I was so fine.

As I sunk deeper into denial and depression, apparently God was there with me on the couch. He'd never left. One day, in a spontaneous burst of determination, I leapt off the couch, strode to the bathroom, flushed all the pills down the toilet, and lay back down. It took no more than a couple of minutes. A handful of breaths. But in that act, I made a reckless decision with no take backs. No backup plan. No plan B. I would survive. Living was plan A, no matter what happened.

I was terrified.

I was at the very bottom. And God's grace met me there. It's weird, really. As we reach the end of ourselves, sometimes we find that God keeps going.

Nothing had changed. My circumstances stayed the same. I went right back on that couch in front of the TV. But something inside me had shifted.

Julie's Story: I Believe I Have Postnatal Depression

A month after my second child was born, I wrote this email to my friend, Lorraine:

Hey, Lorraine, I need to tell you something.

I don't think I can talk about it on the phone because I get a bit teary and choked up when I try talking about it, so I'm emailing you instead.

I believe I have postnatal depression. I don't feel low all the time, but probably 70 percent of the time . . . maybe 80 percent.

I think a lot of it has to do with disrupted sleep and fluctuating hormone levels. But also, if I'm brutally honest, it's also because I am just not a baby/kiddie person, and after a while, mothering makes me feel like I'm going crazy and I just want an escape. I love my kids, but I don't "love" being a mom. I know I'm a good mom, but my heart isn't in it all the time. A lot of the time it feels like a chore—both with Luke and Jess. Luke and Jess are wonderful, so I know that something else is making me feel this way. I'm blaming it on postnatal depression.

It's hard because I'm caring for them every day, all day, and I don't have much time to myself to help bring me back to equilibrium. I'm an introvert. I love having alone time and being by myself for long periods of time, but that doesn't happen when you're a mom to a toddler and a newborn. They suck the life out of you, and you don't get the chance to get that back. It's like a constant drain. It feels so tedious.

I just wish I could take days off. My mom has left now, so I don't get any help anymore. When I think about the future, I get a sinking feeling in my gut. So yeah, that's where I'm at right now. Duane has been really supportive, and I've told him all of this. I've also told my midwife, and she's getting someone who deals with postnatal depression to meet up with me next month. I'm also going to the doctor on Monday.

My mom knows I was struggling with feeling down and depressed. She was really helpful. She was always telling me to look on the bright side and count my blessings. I can do that mentally, but I still feel emotionally low. It's so ridiculous.

Anyway, I will be in touch and hope to see you soon.

> *Luv,*
> *Julie*

—Julie M.

There's pain. There's death. There's depression. There are all these things that grab onto our arms and pull down, down, down toward the floor until we're moving so slowly and then finally sink down in exhaustion. And some people make it and some don't and sometimes the line between living and dead is so thin you can almost see right through it to the other side. These heartbeats inside us that keep beating when we aren't sure we want them to or stop when we do. We feel out of control. We aren't sure how to fix it.

And so we *feel* it. We sit in it together. Life is wacky and unpredictable. Cheers.

The Heart Cry of the Entire Human Race

Sarah: That's not fair!

Jareth: You say that so often, I wonder what your basis for comparison is?

—*Labyrinth*[1]

"It's not fair," my son whined as his eyes filled with tears.

"Yeah, well, life's not fair," I spat back emphatically. And then something inside me broke.

I had just had this conversation with my husband, but instead of decrying the injustice of having to clean my room on a Saturday morning, I was raging about getting royally bleeped by the appraiser for the sale of our home.

Lots of dollars' worth of bleepage. I was turning "it's not fair" into a symphony of pain, complete with whiny strings, blaring brass, moaning woodwinds, and thundering percussion.

As "life's not fair" hurled out my mouth toward my son, I recognized what he sounded like to me, and what I sound like to God. To my son, I'm thinking, *Be thankful you have a room to clean*, and to me, maybe God's thinking, *Be thankful you have a house to sell.* I thought about the millions of people around my city, country, and world who don't have a home about which to sputter and rage.

This is not the first time I've lost perspective.

When I think about unfairness, I think about the daily battle with my kids, but really, it's the heart cry of the entire human race. It's not equal, it's not right, it's broken and twisted and complicated. Our collective lament spirals out to God, and he hears all of it.

And sometimes the injustice or pain seems so monstrous that we have to cry out. We have to scream and tear the air.

Choking on "Supposed"

There are these questions that we answer as kids:

"What do you want to be when you grow up?"
"How many kids do you want to have?"
"Where do you want to live?"
"Who do you want to marry?"

The answers usually morph throughout the years, depending on who came to school on Career Day and who you played M-A-S-H with on the back of the bus on long choir trips. (Wait. Are cool people supposed to bus to sporty things like cross country and soccer? I was on the show choir bus, which took us to competitions where we donned sequined dresses with puffed sleeves and did barrel rolls while singing "Turn the Beat Around.") Inevitably I'd end up in a shack with ten kids and a job as a garbage collector, but I'd be married to my dream hunk, Jeff Goldblum, so at least we had our love.

Via Twitter @UnexpectedMel

Me: What do you want to be when you grow up?
9yo: A teacher.
6yo: A video-game designer.
4yo: Beyoncé.

We make plans and gaze with anticipation into our wide-open future. But so often our ideas pop like broken balloons and heave a sigh of empty air before landing on the floor.

Your parents weren't supposed to get divorced. Your brother wasn't supposed to get sick. Your job wasn't supposed to get eliminated. Your husband wasn't supposed to leave. You weren't supposed to have a miscarriage.

We choke on this word "supposed."

Before we can start to heal, we have to admit what's broken, to admit that we're disappointed. It wasn't supposed to be this way.

MASH

Boys
1.
2.
3.
4.

Careers
1.
2.
3.
4.

Cars
1.
2.
3.
4.

Cities
1.
2.
3.
4.

#of kids
1.
2.
3.
4.

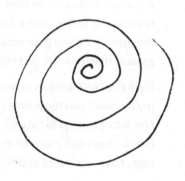

Hey. It's okay to feel disappointed. Do you feel it? *Feel it.* Let yourself.

Megan's Story: I Don't Know Why My Life Took This Turn

The hubs and I got married in November last year, and apparently I missed the entire color guard of red flags before lockin' it in. I knew he had a drug and alcohol addiction from the past when we were dating. I thought it was behind him, and I guess by behind him he meant behind his back . . . and also in the trunk of the car, and hiding in what I now call "the shed of shame," in holes in our yard, the washer and dryer, oh, and don't forget the bag of bedding that was supposed to be for a pet groundhog.

I have extended grace, and grace, and heaps of grace until I thought I was out. Then I ejected my Go-Go-Gadget arms that I never knew I had to extend even more grace only to find that my husband is a big smelly piece of sh . . . poo. Not only is he a big smelly piece of poo, but he wore poo. No, really. He rubbed dog poo on himself one night in an attempt to cover up his marijuana smell so that I wasn't suspicious of him taking a shower at 3 a.m. The story from that night could be a book in itself. I am learning that people with addictions will go to any length to hide their secrets.

As sad as all this is, the only way I can survive is to find the humor in it, and it's not a funny situation. I understand that the man I love and gave vows to is battling something far greater than himself, and I can only watch him get beat.

Over the last eighteen months, I have called the police on my husband countless times, had him arrested twice, ECOed him into a mental facility for a week, seen him go to jail three times. I have lost many of my belongings at the expense of his rage, have separated and filed a protective order. I am now facing the terrifying fact that I can only protect my son but so much as my husband stalks us (oh, yes, complete with binoculars and wearing all black).

Every little thing is painful, but I dig and dig until I can only laugh and shake my head. I was very hush about everything at first, but as things unravel, I have become more open about it, only to find just how many women are in these shoes. It's unbelievable.

I do not know why my life took a turn like this. But now, as I do experience these things and this abuse, I want to reach out to other women in any way that I can. Verbal abuse is not okay. Manipulation is not okay. Physical abuse is most certainly not okay. And being a single momma really does require the village. I could not do this without my mom or my mom friends. Sisterhood is a no-joke kinda thing. In my life, God is the only true thing (am I allowed to call God a thing?) that really can get you through this; mom friends are a very close second. There's no way I could have walked through the last six months of my pregnancy living alone without my best friends keeping my head up. There's no way I could have birthed my sweet son and brought him home to an empty apartment, so my mom stepped in. I am protected at work by other mom friends. They are everywhere. They have become my shield to the crazy. They have walked with me every single painful step of the way. They don't hate my husband because they understand that God did not create him for this and that his soul deserves better. They don't point blame or guilt at me for leaving him, nor do they point it for the times I've wanted to keep working on the marriage only to get smushed again.

Lights at the end of the tunnel aren't always glowing beams of holiness. Sometimes they are forms of confirmation in smelly wads of poop stuck to your husband's shoulder. Um, divorce? Not part of my dream, but at this point in life, yes please.

> Abuse is across the board, across the social ladder, and is really one of the few things that truly seems to tie women of all races, incomes, and backgrounds together (sadly). I think we should be more open about our stuff, be nicer to other women about their stuff, and use it to comfort each other. Life is so hard. We cannot do it without our sisters.
>
> —*Megan D.*

Choose Your Own Adventure

We start out with expectations of how our lives will unfold, right? I had several options, like a *Choose Your Own Adventure* novel with preset endings. All I had to do was make choices along the way and I'd end up at one of three destinations I'd preapproved.

Option 1: My boyfriend would propose, finally. We'd get married, have lots of smoking-hot naked sex, which would inevitably lead to kids or matching his and hers Saab convertibles.

Option 2: My boyfriend would never get his act together. I'd serve God overseas, meet a smoking-hot missionary guy, badabing bada marriage, smoking-hot naked sex, kids.

Option 3: I'd get my MFA in costume design, become a tenured professor, and spend my days up to my eyeballs in fabric with other people's grown kids discussing the ins and outs of wimples and ruffs.

These were my options. And right when I was ready to relegate Option 1 to the cutting-room floor, boyfriend proposed, marriage ensued, and nakedness commenced.

But show me the person whose expectations all come to pass. It's not the way of the world, is it?

1

2

3

4

ROCKSTAR

SCIENTIST

TEACHER

LAWYER

GYMNAST

DOCTOR

PASTOR

ASTRONAUT

Snap your hammy in stage-diving accident. 6 months in body cast.

Exposed to gamma rays in freak lab explosion. Become volatile super-hero.

Recurring nightmare where you're tied up + forced to take scantron tests.

Wardrobe malfunction on national TV in the middle of your floor routine.

On parole + wants to admit paleo is a real thing.

Become a pariah for refusing to be besties. former client gets out

Start reciting lyrics to "Purple Rain" in the middle of closing prayer.

Brain melts

Develop addiction to space. ice cream.

CUT HERE. ASK THE GOOGLE OR ANY 10-YR-OLD GIRL HOW TO FOLD THIS THING.

COOTIE CATCHER

A+ in Waiting Like a Good Christian

When we first got married, I didn't want kids, but then when I did, infertility snuck up into our world quietly, insidiously. The barren months started to choke our joy, and the smoking-hot naked sex became like the trigonometry class that you can't pass and have to take over and over again, just going through the motions and never getting a passing grade. (This illustration only works if you hate math as much as I do.)

Well-meaning friends told us to relax. I turned my peppy punk-rock music up a little louder, danced a little harder, prayed a little deeper. I forced my cheeks into wide smiles as friend after friend announced that she was pregnant. And on the first try? With two different kinds of birth control?

Via Facebook @UnexpectedMel

Evie: When I'm your age, will I get married?

Me: Maybe. That depends on if you find a guy you love.

Evie: I already found a guy!

Me: Who?

Evie: My bear.

Me: Well, he is soft and snuggly, and won't ever argue with you. He might have a hard time getting a job.

Wow. I made jokes about fertility and laughed when people asked if we were "doing it" right and threw baby showers, stitched baby clothes, and knitted fuzzy pastel blankets.

Our conversations would go like this:

Them: Are you guys gonna have kids?

Me: We're working on it. Been struggling with infertility for a few years.

Them: Oh, yeah, me too. I tried for two months to get pregnant and was, like, freaking out that I'd end up infertile and it would be so hard and I was dying, but then I tried herbal tea and it worked that third month. So I totally understand.

Me: (*Just. In. My. Head.*) Yeah you do, pumpkin, yeah you do.

But I was nice. And I checked all the boxes. And I played by the rules. I was earning an A+ in Waiting Like a Good Christian.

And then one day, sitting at church in the balcony, I watched as three of my pregnant friends all entered the sanctuary together, smiling and laughing. They sat down, three baby bumps in a row, and I muttered, "I have to go," to my husband as I ran to the prayer room before the cry-boogers took over my whole face.

Sanctuary means refuge, a safe haven, but in that moment I realized it wasn't anymore. So I stopped going. The church had become a place of torment, a weekly reminder that God hadn't answered my prayer, but it seemed like he'd answered everyone else's. My belief in him didn't falter. I knew he was real. I just really hated his plan. It wasn't fair.

In New Territory

What's your bitter pill sticking to the back of your throat? Maybe it's infertility. Maybe it's cancer. Maybe it's loss of a loved one or your job. Debilitating illness. Divorce. So many of us are devastated, going through life's motions, smiling at church and around the dinner table, and desperately whispering in the depths of our hardening hearts, "It's not fair."

Our expectations meet life's unexpected twists, and our pretty plans are violated and shattered. At first, we try to glue the pieces back together, but it's no good, it's too far gone, and we bury our dreams.

We're disappointed. In new territory. These feelings aren't the fuzzy high we've been conditioned to feel throughout a lifetime of youth group and churchianity. What are the hand motions to the song that will make everything okay again? Where is the upbeat altruism that will pop rock us into a perkier mood? How do we reconcile unfairness with a loving God?

Deep down, we aren't sure if we can trust a God who would let us hurt this badly. That terrifies us, because if we can't trust God, where do we go from here?

Jessica's Story: This Isn't How It's Supposed to Be

Everyone goes into parenthood with a laundry list of expectations. We imagine how our children will look, how they will act, what their personalities will be like. When we (pre-kids) see misbehaving children out in public, we think, "My child will never behave that way." Because, you know, we're all perfect parents before we give birth. With all of those hopes and dreams, I can't think of a single person who desires or prays to have a special-needs child. Even before they're here, we want the very best for our children. We want them to be healthy, happy, and without hardship. It's what we do as mothers—we protect our babies.

When Knox was diagnosed with autism at age two, it was the hardest thing I've ever walked through. My faith was rocked; my expectations were shattered. This was not a part of my plan. I loved him just as fiercely as ever, but with that label came a lot of frustration, anger, and bitterness. I tried my best to just ignore all the things around me that reminded me that Knox was different. It was so much easier to do this when he was little. Because, let's face it, all two and three-year-old boys are loud, hyperactive, and too busy. It started to become more obvious that he was different from other children his age when he was around four. That's when life really started to kick my butt.

Being around other kids Knox's age just about killed me. To know that this is what he "should" be acting like, how he "should" be talking, how he "should" be interacting was more than I could handle as a mother. I felt so angry and broken. I tried my best amidst these feelings to make sure that Knox was getting everything he needed—all the therapy, all the classes, all the services. All of the "stuff" we do for kids who need a little extra help. I loved my boy so much. But some days, I couldn't look at him without seeing AUTISM branded into him.

This summer, everything reached a head. It was a Saturday morning, and Knox was in rare form. He was into everything. Disobedient. Finally, he dumped all of the toilet paper (full rolls) into the guest bathroom toilet. That's when I snapped. I screamed at him. I put him in his room. I screamed at nothing. I locked myself in the bathroom and cried my eyes out. What a failure I was! I sat there and listened to every single lie that Satan whispered in my ear: "You are not enough. God made a mistake. Knox wasn't supposed to be this way—you did something wrong. You'll never be better. It's hopeless. You should not be a mother at all. You are horrible. You're being punished. You are worthy of nothing." I was furious at God, and I let him know it. This was not fair. This could not be my life. This isn't how it was supposed to be.

—*Jessica W.*

A Note About Unfairness

You might be thinking, "No, life's *exactly* fair, and I'm harvesting a crop of exactly what I deserve." Okay, well, there's that. Sometimes we experience consequences for a string of bad choices. If that's you, okay. You can own it. Make the changes you need to make, get out of the situation, find the help you need, come clean. And while you're doing all that hard work, I'm still here, wanting to be your friend. Maybe you're experiencing a long road filled with wrong turns. I'm still sorry. I want to go on this journey with you, whether you're on it because of yourself, other people, or a series of unfortunate events. And a lot of times we have a hodgepodge of all of it, and what came first, egg or chicken? It doesn't really matter. It's all poultry.

How to Fall Apart
Like a Boss

I am amazing at falling apart. I fall apart like a boss. It's a gift, really. In fact, I'm so good at falling apart that I can actually break it down for you into four stages.

Stage One

Decrease showering. One day you get up and think, "I didn't really do anything yesterday that got me sweaty and it's winter and my skin is a little dry anyway, so I'm just going to skip showering today." This is no big deal. What's one day? One day never hurt anyone. Lots of people skip a day of showers, and hey, you'll still change your underwear. You aren't an animal.

A week later, you decide to go for two skipped days. Nothing horrible happened last week when you skipped one. What's one more? Two days back-to-back, no one will notice. It's all good.

You start to have showerless weekends because you aren't really going anywhere or hanging out with anyone, so why not? You're a conservationist. You're saving water. Really, people should thank you. You are so green. Al Gore called to thank you. You're a rock star with the eco-non-showering.

> **Via Twitter @UnexpectedMel**
>
> *Evie: I want to be like you and stay in my jammies every day and never go anywhere.*

Stage Two

You stop finishing sentences. You'll be talking with your kids or spouse or friend or coworker and trail off or just stop. Some examples:

- "I can't find my . . ." Find your what? You can't remember what you lost, but you have a vague sense of incompleteness, like there's something out there you were looking for, but it doesn't matter anymore and you're probably sitting on it and will find it if you ever get off the couch again.
- Describing plans. "I was going to go to the . . ." You don't remember. You don't care. You were going to go somewhere, but it isn't important and you *can't even*. There's home in your jammies eating ice cream in bed, and there's everything else. Everything else is overwhelming.

Stage Three

Binge-watching Netflix. This one is a little murky, because plenty of people binge-watch shows and aren't slowly losing their grip on reality. For them, it's a hobby, like scrapbooking or curling or cosplay. If you're falling apart, this binge-watching is a whole 'nother level. My total breakdown was before the age of Netflix, when we had to invest in a season of something on DVD. I collected all the *Buffys* and *Angels* and The Highlight of My Life was when a new season came out, and I'd spend all weekend watching it.

This is not the problem. IT'S NOT AND YOU CANNOT CONVINCE ME OTHERWISE. This is complete and total awesomesauce. But I should've realized maybe I was crossing a line when I'd seen every episode so many times I could tell you what Buffy was wearing by scene. Falling apart. Like a boss.

Stage Four

You don't notice it at first, but your security food that you save for when you have a really bad day is something you're eating every single day. For me it's Nerds. And as I type this I'm suddenly worried I'm in Stage Four without my knowledge because I'm up to a pack-a-day Nerds habit. Huh. Note to self: take stock of life choices.

The flip side of this is for the stress non-eaters out there, of which I used to be/sometimes still am one: When was the last time you ate a full, balanced meal? Anything at all? Have you eaten today? Please take this book to the kitchen and eat something starchy (see chapter 9, "Comfort Foods That Will Help You Eat Your Feelings," for some awesome recipes). If it's been more than a day or two, please see my original disclaimer and talk to people with letters after their names who can help you get a plan together. I have been there. I am always one meal away from being there. You are not alone.

It's Okay to Fall Apart

I won't insult you by telling you you'll be completely okay, but I will tell you that it's okay to fall apart. Sometimes we have to fall apart. Sometimes it's the healthiest response we can have to life's greatest agonies.

I worry about the people who don't fall apart. Maybe they're fine. Maybe they process differently than I do. Good for them. But I worry that, culturally, we're emotionally constipated. We pound back protein shakes and how-to articles and we erect walls high enough to trap all our ooky monsters into sterilized clean rooms in our souls. We lift and tuck our outside selves when, really, we ought to be sitting in sackcloth and ashes.

The more you force yourself to have it all together on the outside prematurely, the more junk you'll have to power wash off later. Better to fall apart at the beginning and get it over with.

We've lost our ability to lament. And Christians are the worst at this. We freak out if someone isn't embracing all the spunkiest Bible verses and we have a pep talk for every situation.

But there are a lot of verses we ignore, and sometimes it's okay to spend some serious time in a state of lament. Wail, rend your garments (Wear old clothes. Do not rend your Anthro shirt from Christmas. That would make you sadder.), tear your hair (Nope, I don't advise this. Tear some duct tape or something.), and don't try to stuff it for the people around you.

If you need help in this area, look to King David, my emotional Bible muse. The man is a master of lament.

> LORD, do not rebuke me in your anger
>   or discipline me in your wrath.
> Have mercy on me, LORD, for I am faint;
>   heal me, LORD, for my bones are in agony. [*He's swooning; he's got bone problems; this is some serious falling apart. I mean, fainting and bones in agony. He needs a protein shake and some calcium, stat.*]
> My soul is in deep anguish.
>   How long, LORD, how long? [*Deep. The anguish is deep. ARE WE THERE YET? HOW MUCH LONGER?*]
> Turn, LORD, and deliver me;
>   save me because of your unfailing love. [*Because of your love, God, not because of my merit. It's about your character.*]
> Among the dead no one proclaims your name.
>   Who praises you from the grave? [*"So you'd better save me, God, because I can't praise you if I'm dead!" This is solid logic.*]
> I am worn out from my groaning. [*Groaning as a killer cardio routine?*]
> All night long I flood my bed with weeping
>   and drench my couch with tears. [*He is drenching multiple pieces of furniture. He must be dehydrated. And also, EW.*]

My eyes grow weak with sorrow;
    they fail because of all my foes. [*He literally cried his
        eyes out.*]
Away from me, all you who do evil,
    for the LORD has heard my weeping. [*I think everyone
        has heard your weeping, David.*]
The LORD has heard my cry for mercy;
    the LORD accepts my prayer.
All my enemies will be overwhelmed with shame and
    anguish;
    they will turn back and suddenly be put to shame.
    [*Because of his great battle strategy or his amazing
    workout regimen? No. Because he cried and cried out to
    the Lord. So many emotions.*]

Psalm 6

Of course, David had a lot of really good reasons for losing it on a regular basis, whereas my stuff usually consists of things like this:

- My new iPhone is too big for my hand and I can no longer text one-handed under the table where no one can see me.
- Fox canceled *Firefly* a bajillion years ago and I'm still bitter.
- My kids have a permission slip that must be signed or they will never be allowed to cross the threshold of school again or maybe everyone will laugh at them and call them names and they can't find the permission slip and I can't find the permission slip and this field trip is the most important event ever and they can't go and I'm trying to write a note with a crayon because I can't find a pen because I'm not a real grown-up.
- I accidentally drank decaf and can't figure out why I want to take everyone out with a hair straightener on high heat.

You get the idea. No one has tried to kill me. At least not to my knowledge as of the printing of this book.

My friend and her husband had an unexpected, violent death in the family and showed up to church that same morning. We were all like, "WHY ARE YOU HERE!?!" And they said, "Where else would we go? At a time like this, where should we be if not with our church family?"

I was amazed. When I was hurting, I took a breather from the church because I couldn't hide my pain. But my friends ran to the church with their pain. Yes. That's the way to do it. We need church cultures where people feel safe to do this, where we can all sit down together and cry our eyes out, just like King David.

When you feel like you're falling apart, sometimes the bravest thing you can do is wake up, open your eyes, exhale, and get out of bed. Sometimes the hardest, bravest thing is choosing to live another day in this broken, wonderful world.

Every morning when my alarm goes off and that crushing sense of reality descends on my chest, I roll over to stare at the ceiling, throw my hands open, palms up, and say, "God, thank you for another day. I invite you into it." Even when I'm not sure I believe what I'm saying.

Digging Out from a Good Wallow

Guy Fleegman: I'm not even supposed to be here. I'm just "Crewman Number Six." I'm expendable. I'm the guy in the episode who dies to prove how serious the situation is. I've gotta get outta here.

—*Galaxy Quest*[1]

Sometimes after you fall apart, you just need to wallow. There is no shame in this, and when done correctly, it's part of the healing process. But you can't park your buffalo in the wallow too long; sooner or later you have to get up and lumber about. So here are my general phases for digging out and not letting things get wonky.

Phase One

Give yourself a day. Wallow. Let yourself eat Swedish fish out of the family-sized bag and watch *Legally Blonde* one more time and follow it up with *Die Hard*. Binge-watch *The Walking Dead* and develop an unexplainable crush on Daryl Dixon. (This is JUST A HYPOTHETICAL EXAMPLE. I in no way experienced this and know nothing about this greasy bowhunter. He means absolutely nothing to me. WHAT. I JUST CARE ABOUT THIS PRECIOUS BABY MAN SO MUCH AND NEED HIS HEART TO BE OKAY. And I worry that by the time this book comes out, he will have already been eaten by zombies, and I'll be devastated. Whatever, he means nothing to me. I'm fine.)

Give yourself a day. But no more than a day. As someone who

spent half her twenties on the couch, please hear me on this. One day. Okay, maybe three. A week, tops.

Confession: After I lost our last in vitro embryos and knew there wouldn't be any more, I read all four *Twilight* books in one week. DO NOT JUDGE ME. Okay, maybe judge me a little. That's fair.

I had so many emotions, and I wasn't ready to deal with any of them. Hey, rather than finding myself at the bottom of a bottle, I found myself inside the head of a high school girl. I have no memories from that week except who was Bella going to choose, Edward or Jacob, and what if the Volturi came and wiped them out, and what would I do if I became a vampire? Would I live in Forks or maybe a fancy island in the middle of the Pacific where my skin could glitter as much as I want and no one would care?

I wallowed for a week, avoided all my feelings, and then finally came up for air, where the devastating loss was waiting right where I left it.

Via Facebook @UnexpectedMel

Having to get up at the cracky-pants of dawn this week to get Ana to camp, and I see why morning people feel morally superior to us night owls. I'm getting in a whole day's worth of work before 8:30 a.m. . . . and a whole day's worth of caffeine. This schedule is seriously messing with my late-night *Battlestar Galactica* marathons.

Phase Two

Now it's time to go outside and take yourself on a walk or go to a coffee shop. Grieve sitting up. It's the same as lying down in bed, but you're wearing actual clothing (albeit the yoga variety) and sitting in public. You can still be by yourself, but you're feeling the energy and hearing the coffee grinder and sharing air with other people. It's a start. You can hang here for as long as you need. Try making small talk with the person next to you. Read a funny book. Wait, no, I mean, read this book. But once you've read it, read something funny that's filled with other messy people. Avoid clean people. Avoid liars. You can't take too much of the life-together liars right now. Block them on Twitter and hide them on Facebook. Set Pinterest on fire. Break Instagram with a sledgehammer. You do not need other people's filtered perfection right now.

Phase Three

Text a friend and hang out. Safe friends only. Let her or him know upfront if you don't want to talk about the thing, and if this person can't abide that, then this is not your phase-three friend. You need someone who will respect your electric fence with the razor wire on top and just be content to sit next to you and bump shoulders. Talk about easy stuff and laugh about inappropriate things. Laughing about inappropriate things always makes me feel better. If I'm in the hospital, bring me a whoopee cushion and every double entendre joke about balls in your arsenal. Do not bring me flowers.

It's Going to Be Sor-kay

It's going to be sor-kay. Sort of okay. I have no idea how I know this or how it's going to be sor-kay, but I know it will be. Somehow. You will survive. You will learn to smile again. You will remember what's important. You will love and you will live and you may even love living. And if you have a terminal cancer diagnosis and I just told you that you will live, feel free to face punch me now.

For the rest of you facing absolutely horrifying, though probably nonfatal, loads of crappery, channel your inner Gloria Gaynor. You will survive. Even if you don't really want to.

Complaint as a Spiritual Discipline

Mary Katherine Gallagher: Oh my God!

Jesus: Oh my Me! How are you?

Mary Katherine Gallagher: It's going okay.

—*Superstar*[1]

Dear God,

You aren't really being fair by letting all my friends have babies and me not have them. They're complaining because it took two months to get pregnant and how hard the waiting was, and then the commercial on TV with that annoying perfect person said, "Because when you decide to have a baby, nine months is long enough to wait," and I wanted to hurt her, like maybe stick her toothbrush in the toilet or beat her with a shoe. In a Christian way.

I don't really understand. Lots of people who don't want babies get pregnant, and I really, really want a baby and can't. That is some kind of whacked-out system, God. I mean that as respectfully as possible. I love you. And argh.

It seems like with the kids-having thing, it's always about trust with you. My friends getting pregnant by breathing on each other while using two forms of birth control and being between jobs are having to trust you to provide financially, and Alex and I with a job and a house and a room for the baby and lots of free time are having to trust you for the baby. Why do you do that? Always with the lessons in trust.

So. I trust you. I don't like it. But I'm trusting. In a constipated kind of way.

Love, Melanie

61

Dear God,
    You aren't really being fair by _____
_____.
I don't really understand because _____
_____.
You seem to be _____.
Why are you doing that?
I'm frustrated. But.
I trust you. __yes__ __no__

I love you. __yes__ __no__

_____
your name

Part of the Fun of Life

Life is a weird little thing, isn't it? We spend so much of our days just trying to get to the next thing, cross the thing off the list, make it to the weekend. It goes by, and if you're anything like me, part of the fun of life is complaining about it.

Maybe I'm not supposed to admit that in a book. What I meant to say was, part of the fun is counting your blessings and trusting God. Yep. That's totally what I meant.

No, for realsies, I enjoy complaining. A good rant really cleanses the pores and makes you feel bought in to the whole thing. Really demonstrates you have skin in the game.

Maybe complaining could be a spiritual discipline. One of the lesser-known spiritual disciplines. Could complaining be healthy? . . . Nope. No. I just Googled it, and the Bible people have a lot to say about complaining being the opposite of what we're supposed to do. Drat.

Okay, so maybe we're not supposed to just walk around griping about life, but I do think we can purge our feelings in a healthy way. Throughout Psalms, David shared his fears and worries and all his feelings about how things were going. He ranted it all out to God, and then he always came around at the end with some kind of declaration of trusting God. So maybe complaining *to God* is totally kosher.

> I cry aloud to the LORD;
>> I lift up my voice to the LORD for mercy.
> I pour out before him my complaint;
>> before him I tell my trouble.
>
> *Psalm 142:1–2*

God Can Handle Your Emotions

Lemme tell you something about prayer. The most important thing about prayer is to be totally honest with God. God can handle your emotions. He can handle all of it. He knows what's going on anyway, and you'll feel better if you just get it all out. I feel like when I pour everything out to God and get really honest with him, even if it's painful and completely unflattering, then God says, "Okay. Now we're getting somewhere. I can work with this."

Via Unexpected.org
August 4, 2010

I'm so grateful to serve a God who can handle my discontent. And oohhh, how I am so discontented right now with the pain in the world. I've had some harsh words for God these past few weeks. I'm so glad he can handle it. He can absorb my anger and frustration. He's strong enough to let me beat my fists against his mighty chest over and over, flailing and kicking and sobbing in anger. Why, God? Why, why, why?!?! I can't see it. I can't see your plan. Are these kids collateral damage in your cosmic battle? And I can screech at him with all my human ferocity, and I know that he's God. He can handle it. He can handle how ticked off I am. In fact, I think he put a bunch of pleading, griping, and bullying in his Word to show us how to let him have it. So today, I'm giving him everything I have, all my crap, screaming at him, punching at him, but running *to* him. Because if I can't take all this angst to God, who can I take it to?

As a parent, I see this with my kids. I can tell when they're hurting. I can definitely tell when they're mad at me. Sometimes they stomp to their rooms and slam the doors. One of my kiddos likes to slam the door, open it, check to see if I noticed, then slam it again just to make sure I got the point. They glare and refuse to make eye contact and it's the absolute worst.

But then. After time. Eventually they start talking, and at first it's angry accusations, "Why won't you let me . . . ?!?" "How could you . . . ?!?!" "IT'S NOT FAIR!!!!!" They rage at me, but they still know that I'm the boss and in charge. And somewhere inside of them, they know that I can help make it better. I'm the subject of their anger and also their helper and rescuer and comforter. So on the other side of the rage, they make eye contact, I hold them, and they relax in my arms. Okay. Now we're getting somewhere. I can work with this. (It seems that some teens spend several years in the rage stage before the hug stage. Which is also kinda true for some of us with God.)

Via Unexpected.org
August 10, 2010

Lately, I have let God have it—my frustration, my impatience, the general *ARGH*-ocity of my inner grump. I've yelled like Habakkuk, crying out:

> How long, LORD, must I call for help,
>> but you do not listen?
> Or cry out to you, "Violence!"
>> but you do not save?
> Why do you make me look at injustice?
>> Why do you tolerate wrongdoing?
> Destruction and violence are before me;
>> there is strife, and conflict abounds.
> Therefore the law is paralyzed,
>> and justice never prevails.
> The wicked hem in the righteous,
>> so that justice is perverted.
>
> *Habakkuk 1:2–4*

I've lost my inner woo-hoo and found myself swept away by the dismal undertow of despair. I've criticized God for not rescuing more, for not stepping up like I know he can. Too much corruption, too much pain and suffering, too many deaths and sunken, hopeless eyes. My faith is still solid, but *eek*, my patience is wearing thin.

And as I've sat exhausted, after pounding God's chest with my little fists and looking defiantly up at him through tear-scorched eyes, I've found the comfort of a Father who's grieving with me, who hates it more than I do. And I've felt something return to me as I've flopped down in surrender.

Hope.

Hope in who I know God is. Hope in his character. Hope in his plan. Hope in his promises. And this week I'm looking through fresh, smile-crinkled eyes at the work that he's doing around me. I see it. I see him.

The Swear Shed

Matthew 6:6 talks about going into your room and closing the door when you pray instead of being a total diva about it in front of everyone. The KJV calls it a "closet," and thus birthed the tradition of Christians talking about going into their prayer closets. I don't really have a prayer closet. Mine is more of a swear shed. Hey, guys, I'm headed out to the shed.

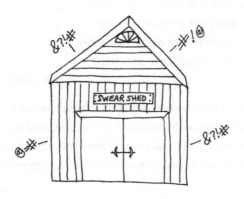

I think there's a way to approach God both reverently and honestly, fully yourself where you are. And I think our man David has modeled that for us.

> How long, LORD? Will you forget me forever? [*The man is accusing God of forgetting him. And he's kinda sarcastic about it, right? In my head, he's totally sarcastic.*]
>
> How long will you hide your face from me?
>
> How long must I wrestle with my thoughts
>
> and day after day have sorrow in my heart? [*Playing the guilt card, for sure. My kids try this one on me about Disney World. How long must we be the only ones who haven't gone? How long, Mom?*]
>
> How long will my enemy triumph over me?
>
> Look on me and answer, LORD my God. [*He's begging God for an answer, maybe demanding one. Definitely telling God what to do. Look how direct he is here. There's no tiptoeing or groveling here. But boy howdy, he calls him "Lord my God." So there's reverence.*]
>
> Give light to my eyes, or I will sleep in death,
>
> and my enemy will say, "I have overcome him,"
>
> and my foes will rejoice when I fall. [*Fix this now, or I'll die and my enemies will win and you'll look bad because they know I follow you! Well played, David, wellll playyyyed.*]
>
> But I trust in your unfailing love;
>
> my heart rejoices in your salvation. [*There it is. All this other stuff. This freaking out and then, "but I trust. Your love doesn't fail, even though you aren't answering in my timing. I trust you. Your love doesn't fail. And I'm celebrating your salvation, even in this hard time."*]
>
> I will sing the LORD's praise,
>
> for he has been good to me. [*He has been. David remembers. He keeps singing. He keeps praising. Because of the has been.*]
>
> *Psalm 13*

68 | All the Feels

So that's what I try to do. Rant, complain, freak out all over God, then trust. In *One Thousand Gifts*, Ann Voskamp writes,

> I make soup and I bake bread and I know my supreme need is joy in God and I know I can't experience deep joy in God until I deep trust in God. I shine sinks and polish through to the realization that trusting God is my most urgent need.

If I deep trusted God in all the facets of my life, wouldn't that deep heal my anxiety, my self-condemnation, my soul holes?

The fear is suffocating, terrorizing, and I want the remedy, and it is trust. Trust is everything.[2]

Via Twitter @UnexpectedMel
Me: Let's do highs and lows.
Elliott: I'll start. Is "#%@!" a bad word?
Me: Yep, yes it is.
#familydinner

A Note About Trust

I cannot just force myself to trust God. You don't have to do that, make yourself trust God. Trust can't be forced. I can't force myself to trust anyone, and if things are going not your way and you have a lot going on that's not really inspiring confidence in a loving, caring God, then trust may be a long way away from the truth.

So don't trust God. Ask him to help you trust him. Seriously, if all the good stuff comes from him, if he's the root of everything, and there are all these beautiful fruity things we're supposed to feel and exude, then don't waste your time trying to be trusting. Ask him to give you some trust. Put it back on him. Let him give you the ability to trust him. That's not on you. You're just supposed to abide. Just hang out and let him do the work in you (John 15:4).

So Totes Righteously Angry on Your Behalf

Michelle: Listen up, you little spazoids. I know where you live and I've seen where you sleep. I swear to everything holy that your mothers will cry when they see what I've done to you.
—*Tommy Boy*[1]

Don't you love the friend who gets angry for you? If you're tired or feeling glum and life kicked you in the stomach, but you're too deflated to even work up some anger, it feels amazing when a friend puts on a good rant for you. Well, in this chapter, I am so totes righteously angry on your behalf. (A note about "totes": I started using this ironically about a year ago and recently realized, to my complete horror and shame, that I just plain use this term now. Totally. Totes. There's not a lot to say. I'm sorry, and the one thing keeping me going is knowing that I can use this whenever I need to embarrass my kids in front of their friends. "Hey, guys! You totes scarfed up an entire jumbo box of Popsicles. Awesomesauce. So sick.")

Got fired? HOW DARE THEY.

He dumped you? WHAT AN IDIOT.

Cancer came back? THERE IS NOT ENOUGH RAGE IN THE UNIVERSE FOR WHAT I'M FEELING FOR YOU RIGHT NOW.

Your teen snuck out and got a multi-colored tattoo of all four Teenage Mutant Ninja Turtles on his upper thigh? HULK SMASH.

You stay calm and be an adult. I got this. RAAAA-ARRRRRRRR!!!!!!!!

Everyone knows what anger feels like. I didn't think I was a big anger kind of person, but then I got kids and they started talking back to me and flipping their hair around and oh. I know anger.

> **Via Twitter @UnexpectedMel**
>
> *Ana: Mom, when I say duh to you, I'm just answering yes in Russian.*
>
> *Me: Nice try. Da is yes in Russian. Duh is teenager for You're a moron.*

In the Christian world, we talk about "righteous anger," like when Jesus overturned the tables in the temple because people were selling stuff in God's house. Righteous Jesus-style anger is supposed to be a-okay, whereas the rest of us losing our crap on each other is not acceptable in the anger department.

Which is too bad, because Alex and I can get spectacularly angry. But never at the same time. Thank goodness, the planet is safe.

Ruined Beyond Repair

This winter we decided to road trip to Kentucky to see my aunt and uncle and my grandmother. None of them had met Ana yet, and also they are fantastic and I missed them. Both fortunately and unfortunately, Big Winter decided to dump his whole load up on the South, and while our kids made snow angels outside, Alex and I checked reports and figured out how to get home.

We decided to go around Nashville, since Tennessee was in a state of emergency and the city looked like one big interstate pileup. As we turned off the highway onto a smaller road, I accidentally told Alex to turn at the wrong light. And then I accidentally suggested he just turn around in a little unplowed driveway.

And then we accidentally got stuck and felt our wheels spin and spin. We were delightfully suspended in a van with our kids on an unknown road in the middle of a state emergency.

Raised-in-Detroit and Raised-in-Cleveland had gotten stuck in the snow like a couple of Southerners. So that was humbling. But not yet. First the anger, then the humility.

Like I said, Alex and I are well-matched in the freak-out department. He freaks out about big stuff, and I freak out about little things. As soon as our tires started spinning, I went into calm, serene mode while he used All The Words and punched the window. It was like I was shot up with the mother lode of Valium, and he was hulking out.

The next part was out of a movie. I always wondered why country guys needed ginormous pickup trucks. Were they compensating for something? Was it for country boy cred? I now know it's for pulling snotty, helpless minivan drivers out of the messes they make. Guys in beefy pickup trucks showed up like angels and dug around our tires and attached winches and towed us out with their huuuuge johnsonmobiles. Go, country boys. Go, country trucks. I'm a believer.

Alex and I settled back down in silence as we made our way down the street. Several miles later, we finally made eye contact and started laughing. I cracked a joke about All The Words and waited to see if he'd laugh or punch the window again. He cracked a joke right back and we were fine.

And then we stopped for lunch and Alex opened the back of the van and all the teddy bears collected on our travels exploded onto the dirty, wet parking lot of Taco Bell. He announced, "The bears are ruined. They're ruined beyond repair." He kept up with this overly dramatic diatribe as he threw the bears back in the van. Every time he threw a bear in, it would knock the other ones out. He did this at least three times before coming up with a new plan, all while cursing the Taco Bell parking lot. The kids started fake crying and I was in my own reality show, a show about an overly dramatic family tested to their limits on the outskirts of snowy Nashville.

I decided to stare at my phone and pretend I wasn't there, and right then I got an email from my *Coffee+Crumbs* editor, Ashlee, about a TV producer interested in interviewing me for a reality show about mommy bloggers. As if reality TV needs more families losing their junk on one another in public. The entire scene was so absurd that I felt a deep snort-laugh forming somewhere deep in the bowel region.

Alex finished bagging the Ruined Beyond Repair stuffed animals (They're fine. I washed them. I don't want to worry you.) and sat back in the driver's seat. He reached for a can of Coke Zero that had been frozen in the car all weekend. It exploded in his hands. And I focused all my attention on not laughing.

Sometimes Anger Feels Good

Wait, I got so into that story that I forgot why I was telling you. Oh, yeah, anger. Sometimes when you're going through something awful, you get angry. Angry at the doctors, angry at your family, angry at your boss, angry at the guy. And sometimes anger feels good, at least for a little while.

Good friends know how to let you be angry and get it all out. They let you process the emotions. They get angry with you and rage on your behalf. They say things like, "I can't believe he did that to you!" and "What a jack-wad!" And sometimes, when you're totally calm, they get angry for you.

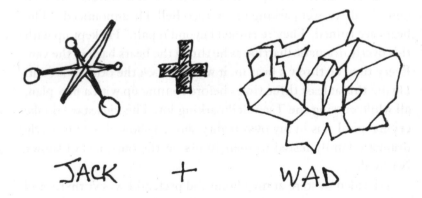

JACK + WAD

And then good friends calm and soothe you and don't leave you in a frothing rage. I have a couple of friends I text when I'm raging. They rage back on my behalf, then ask, "How can I help?" Then they say they'll pray for me. And because they're good friends, I believe them.

When my kids come home from school angry over an injustice, like they

> **Via Twitter @UnexpectedMel**
>
> *Elliott: Evie is mimicking me.*
>
> *Evie: No, I'm not. I'm copying you.*
>
> *Elliott: Mimicking IS copying.*
>
> *Alex: Way to know your synonyms.*
>
> *Evie: Way to know your synonyms.*

had to miss recess because another kid was talking to them and got them in trouble or so-and-so pushed them on the bus and made them fall in front of everyone and didn't even get in trouble, I try to do the same thing. Get angry with them. I don't say "jack-wad," though, because my kids don't need any more words. They have enough already. And then I soothe them, ask them how I can help, and pray. (And ask them to think about forgiving the person, not because that person deserves it but because it'll make them feel better. Forgiveness is cool like that.)

You're going to have angry days. Real burning anger. Ask yourself why you're angry. Ask yourself who made you angry. Is it a person, a situation, God?

Alex and I stress each other out when we're dumping anger on each other, so one thing we've started doing that helps is identifying these things out loud. I'll start to rage about something and say, "I know I sound angry. I am. I'm not mad at you. I'm mad at the situation." And that'll help him feel less defensive and more, "Yes, the situation does blow chunks, and I'm totally with you."

As we've been wrapping our heads around the diagnoses for our family, we've been stretched as therapists, neuropsychologists, psychiatrists, and educators have overloaded us with information, strategies, and treatments. We see our kids struggling, and all our available understanding is funneling to them, leaving precious little for each other. A few weeks ago we found ourselves screaming at each other in the car about . . . I have no idea, and then Alex's voice tore and out came, "It's so hard, feeling this burden for your child. Even though it's not your fault, you feel responsible for such pain." The anger melted into helplessness, which slid into togetherness.

Grrrr . . . ateful

When I catch myself running around angry and it doesn't want to abate and it feels like the anger is starting to camp out on my front lawn, I turn to gratitude. Gratitude puts anger in its place every time.

1. I'm grateful that I get to be really angry on this comfy couch.
2. I'm grateful for this chocolate I'm eating while I'm angry.
3. I'm grateful for Marvel Studios.

It's really hard for me to start being grateful, but once I pop the cork off the bottle, the thankfulness starts bubbling out. My problems don't go away, but my perspective changes. Sometimes I like being angry. Sometimes it feels good. For a little while. But we can't rage forever, and at some point we have to face if we're being angry or if we're an angry person.

Channel your inner Ann Voskamp and count the gifts. Gratitude reminds me of sit-ups. Sit-ups are the worst when you first start doing them. You feel like your stomach is going to burn right out of your body and somehow everything hurts—your back, your neck, your butt. It's awful. And you can never keep up with the stupid workout video or teacher at the gym. And you worry the fart you have locked and loaded from this morning's Kashi cereal is going to jet right out of your shorts. The first few crunches are killers. But then after

Via Twitter @UnexpectedMel

Sweating in 94 degrees and 4yo wants to wear me like a skin suit. I swear I'm a better parent when I'm not hot.

#pleasegetoffme
#idontwanttocuddle

a while, over time, they get easier. Gratitude is clearly the exact same as this. It's hard, everything hurts, and then eventually it feels more natural, and you find you can do a bunch of gratitudes without breaking a sweat or sharting yourself.

Darlene's Story: I Surrender

I was a girl who fell in love with a sweet man at the age of twenty-three. We had dreams. We had to plow through life at a crazy pace to make those dreams evolve. Some did and some did not.

Flash ahead to twenty-three years into the marriage. I was a senior account executive of an awesome company that I loved. My husband was a VP of a bank. We had three gorgeous daughters—ages fourteen, twelve, and four. We were involved in church, soccer, and Girl Scouts. We were the pretty family that from the outside looked like we had so many blessings. Internally, we were dying a slow death, yet we were so busy with pursuits and trappings that we could not even see it taking place, slow and precise. I believed in God, but I placed him in a box and brought him out when I felt it necessary. We didn't truly "walk" with him, and all that was about to become blatantly apparent.

I went in for a routine Ob-Gyn check. I was sitting there annoyed that my day was being taken up when my OB looked at me as she felt something odd. I had been too busy to really look after myself. I was running a career, a household, and raising kids. I was sent down the road for an immediate mammogram. No big deal probably.

I left that office with a card for the next week for a biopsy. Tearful and frightened, I started to process options, scenarios, and dilemmas. I called my husband, who believed it was no big deal, so I went to the biopsy alone. I left with a Stage 1 diagnosis, a surgery date, and a treatment plan—the beginning of a new journey. I called the women in my small group, asked them to pray, and took my God out of his box, but instinctively I could feel change all around. Deep down I knew something was still to hit.

Two weeks after my surgery, on Christmas Eve, after an anger-filled argument, my husband told me that this was it. There was no more "us." For the first time in my life, I had no control, no fix, no answers. I waited a week before even sharing the news, thinking it was just one of those empty threats. I prayed for hours on end. Surely God would fix this. I was waiting for a miracle. I told God that this could be his story of redemption and restoration, but the quiet was muffling, and in hindsight it was just that. It was part of the path for my own personal redemption and restoration. I just was naïve enough to think that I knew better what the outcome "should" be.

As I entered into treatment and radiation, moved my husband out, and watched my life fall to shreds, I cried. Daily. Almost every hour. The pain was too great to bear, and I just asked God to take me. I had no will to live anymore. I was NOT de-signed to carry all this. The failure of a marriage, the heartache of my children, the disappointment of my family . . . I moved from being sad to being Mad as Hades. SCREAMED at God. My prayer closet became the shower, for I could weep and scream and the sound of the water would drown out the noise so that my children could not hear. Then on one late-night rampage, God and I had this talk.

The one where I was hacked at what he had given me. My divorce was going to happen. My burns from radiation were hurting. My children were falling apart. My home was falling into shambles with repairs, messes, things I had no clue how to fix. Why, oh why, if he loved me so much, would this be my path? And in the moment when I had cried so hard, screaming, kneeling, beating my fists on the carpet, and I lay there exhausted trying to catch my breath, I heard this voice so clear telling me, "JUST LET GO. LET IT ALL GO. LET ME HANDLE THIS—I WILL TAKE THIS AND I WILL MAKE GOOD OF IT, GIVE YOU THE LIFE YOU DESERVE TO LIVE, AND I WILL TAKE CARE OF THOSE YOU LOVE TOO. JUST TRUST. BUT YOU HAVE TO LET GO." I opened my eyes and no one was there.

That night I surrendered. I burned the box I had kept my Lord in for all my life. I shared every minute and every mess with him, and my path changed dramatically.

I began again. I surrendered each morning. And each night. Some days were better than others. I sought to heal from my reality and took responsibility for my part. Yes, it was unfortunate timing that my husband left me in the health crisis I had, but I can't speak for his path, battles, and struggles. He and God continue to work through that just as I continue to work on reframing my own personal walk in faith.

I was such a control freak. Appearances meant a lot. When you are standing in front of everyone you pass in tattered shards and your circumstances bear what your reality truly is, there are no such things as appearances anymore. I let go every day. I only want the work that Christ has done in my life getting me through to be the main story of my circumstances. The tsunami that year did not end with my cancer, with my divorce. It also included my oldest contemplating suicide because her pain was so great, the death of my mom (she died the day my divorce was signed by the judge), and the loss of my career.

Through it all I give thanks for what I have before me. I commit to continue on with my circumstances and have God walk with

me. And most importantly for someone like me, I surrender.
I LET GO.

I did not really start living until I lost it all. The pretty life had
to go and all the trimmings with it for me to see. I am grateful
God came for me. My struggles now are very different—my
perspective of what is important, being a single mom with
mucho teenage angst, to date or not to date, how to divide
time into chunks that are intentional and matter. I am grateful,
as a stray, that God found me, claimed me, cleaned me up, and
gave me the life he did plan for me. I can't say how things will
all end up—just that he will be with me through everything
good, crazy, chaotic, and bad.

—*Darlene F.*

-PART-
THREE

Coping Mechanisms for the Horribly Mangled

Because When Life Throws You Under the Bus, You Can't Just Lie There Forever.

Fighting Emotional Gangrene

Xander: Well, I guess it could be worse. I could have gangrene on my face.

—Buffy the Vampire Slayer[1]

I've seen gangrene up close. The second time I visited Uganda, I took a group of people with me, including my dad and a fourteen-year-old girl named Ansley in my high school small group at church. We were visiting the kids we sponsor through HopeChest (more about that in chapter 21) and seeing the new meeting hall and kitchen they'd built, and as we played with the kids and talked with the local leaders of the community, Ansley got to know a little five-year-old girl named Betty (name changed). The first thing we noticed about Betty was her smile. She could light up all of northern Uganda with that smile. The second thing we noticed was her arm. Hot porridge had spilled on her forearm and Betty was in a lot of pain. She hid her wound under a dirty rag and shrieked defiantly when the other kids would poke it.

Over here in our world, with a Rite Aid and CVS on every corner, this would've been an easy fix. You burn your arm, you smear it with any ointment ending in -sporin and you move on with your life. But Betty didn't have Magicsporin, and her wound grew and grew until it took over her arm and threatened her life.

Her new friend Ansley did what good friends do—she noticed her pain. Good friends notice and do something about it. She brought Betty to me. And I did what I've done with boo-boos my whole life. I brought her to my dad. He's a veterinarian, and

Betty wasn't a puppy but we weren't a medical team, so the vet got to work getting the gangrene out, and Betty's arm began to heal. It was slow and painful work, and she was so brave. Every day, they worked the gangrene out together, while she held on to her friend Ansley for support, and little by little, the smell went away, the rotten flesh was replaced with healthy skin, and Betty was whole again.

When we don't deal with our feelings, they can get gangrenous just like Betty's arm. And fighting emotional gangrene is slow, painful work too.

Here's the thing. No one can tell you to love your life. No one can tell you that you'll get on the other side of this and smile again. You don't believe it when you're going through something horrible. You can't know for sure. And your thing is different from anybody else's thing, so flurf all of us with our survival stories of God's great faithfulness.

All we can do is share stories of our own survival and how we cope along the way. It might not be your survival and it might tick you off. But time and again I've seen this thing that happens when someone encounters something terrible, slowly inches through the horrible thing, and learns how to breathe again. There are scars and they might be horribly mangled and bruised, but they made it to the other side. We need to hear these stories, to know that survival in the face of badness is possible. And not just survival, but sur-thrival. We can be wounded and thrive. And we can be cheesy and make up words like sur-thriving.

There's a Process

Time is important for healing, but time isn't the only thing. So is what you do with the time.

If you shove everything in a tiny box and sliver it up into your spleen like an evil splinter and never speak of it or air it out or take it for a walk, someday you'll be like those people who find out a surgeon accidentally sewed up some gloves and rags and a dead rat inside them after a routine hysterectomy and they didn't know what was wrong until everything started festering and oozing. Festering AND oozing. It isn't pretty, people. It isn't healthy. Healing takes time and it takes dealing with what's inside you. You have to open up your guts and get the bad stuff out. Emotional gangrene won't take care of itself. Some coping mechanisms—like sharing your story—help you heal. But some—like substance abuse or too much shopping or having sex with everybody—just make you fester.

So maybe it's counseling or your close group of friends or your pastor or your really good listener of a spouse or journaling or prayer mixed with yoga or all of the above on a rotation. There's a process, an ugly, beautiful, awful, cathartic process that has to happen to get to the other side. The question isn't "Why did the chicken cross the road?" but "How did he cross it?" Figure out how you're going to cross it and commit to the process.

Kristy's Story: Grieving Together

Leave it to Disney . . . Months and months after my second miscarriage, I thought I'd fully grieved my loss, but my husband hadn't seemed to. My husband and I watched *Up*, forgetting that the first scene depicts Ellie and Carl getting pregnant, then being devastated when they miscarried. After the movie, we held each other, sobbed profusely, and for the first time really grieved our losses together.

—*Kristy B.*

The Grace-Bearers

Find the grace-bearers in your life. These are the people with whom you can be disgusting and they offer you grace and forgiveness. You don't abuse these people. They are human beings and they love you. But you aren't afraid to be gross in their presence.

Last year I was hit by an SUV right on the driver's side. I was taking dinner to a friend who'd had a baby and when my van got slammed between two cars, the food exploded everywhere. I heard myself screaming and screaming and thought I was covered in my own warm, viscous guts, but it turned out that it was just baked ziti and my guts were all still exactly where they should be. I spent the evening in the hospital and at the beginning it wasn't bad, smelled kinda good, but as the hours dragged on, the ziti started to sour and by the end, I was definitely the smelliest person there. It's humbling, sitting in a wheelchair all night amidst strangers, smelling like rotten food with ziti guts dangling from my clothes and in between my toes. At first, I was saying, "It's ziti, not blood," and by the end I was saying, "It's rancid ziti, not vomit." I ended up in physical therapy for months. And I can't stand ziti anymore.

And then during that whole thing, I had my entire lower gums grafted and a frenectomy. I couldn't talk. I couldn't eat. I couldn't turn my head or use my left arm or lift anything and my jaw was swollen and made me look like Gaston from *Beauty and the Beast*. My whole body hurt. It was painful and I worried I'd be messed up forever and I was stressing because part of my job is talking and I love talking. I felt like a shell of myself. My entire personality was gone. I couldn't smile, so my snarky sense of humor got me in trouble. When I'd say something kinda awful and pair it with my big smile, the humor worked, but when I couldn't smile I just came off like a jerknut over and over. People wanted to know what was wrong. I was miserable.

And I'd show up to physical therapy every other day and watch the man who had lost his leg in an accident and the little girl whose leg turned the wrong way work hard without complaint, and I knew beyond a shadow of a doubt that I was an overdramatic wimp.

The Poor Baby

But still, I went through a rough patch. And my mom and my husband kept giving me grace. They saw me at my worst. At one point when I was spewing bile, my mom just looked at me, waved her hand, smiled a bit, and said, "Okay, stop talking." They offered love and unconditional acceptance. They reminded me what grace was. My attitude was so awful that I deserved to be shunned, to be put out of the camp with my leprous attitude. Instead they brought me mushy foods and told me, "Poor baby."

Poor baby is something my mom has used my entire life. As an adult, I text her now and say, "I need a 'poor baby.'" And she texts back with lots of emojis, as good moms do.

Poor baby was never condescending or belittling. It wasn't done sarcastically (most of the time). It was my mom's way of entering into my pain, acknowledging it, and giving me a minute to bum out.

And then the minute was over and it was back to work, back to life, back to reality. She was good like that, grieving with me but not letting it consume me. I probably would've been fine if she'd moved in with me during the whole infertility thing. See, we should never, ever leave our moms. (Somewhere a Christian marriage counselor just lost his wings. Kids, clap loudly to make the marriage counselor fly again and chant, "I do believe in leaving and cleaving!")

Via Unexpected.org
January 28, 2013

In Isaiah 42:14, God compares himself to a woman in childbirth, so we know that God the Father is also motherly. When I think about my wounds, these owies needing a soft touch and tenderness, I wonder at the God of the universe as Healer, the mother with the first aid kit stocked with Band-Aids and

Neosporin for the soul. Will the Creator of the universe, who makes the earth melt and the mountains crumble into the sea, hold me and rock me and whisper "poor babies" in my ear?

The Fuzzy Blanket

There are grace-bearers with comforting words, but then as much as they love us, they can't be with us all the time. And we wouldn't want them to be. Sometimes we have to work these things out alone, for a little while, and then the people come back.

For the times when you can't have your person, you need a fuzzy blanket. This is not stupid. This is therapeutically critical for your sur-thrival process. Fuzzy blankets are my favorite. I wrap up in one every night, and I travel with one, and not just because Alex likes to crank the air conditioning in the car even in the dead of winter. At the beach house in the summer, I walk around in my fuzzy blanket womb, and I brought it to foster care training last year because sitting in a room of strangers all weekend listening to stories of child abuse makes me need a fuzzy blanket more than ever. I've given my kids fuzzy blankets, and for his birthday this year, I gave Alex a Pac-Man fuzzy blanket. Sometimes when a friend goes through something hard, I bring her a fuzzy blanket. (Say fuzzy blanket one more time, Melanie.)

It's like a hug that you can curl up in all day. If someone you know is struggling, and you don't know what to say, and you don't know how to help, you can always just show up with a fuzzy blanket. It's like a *poor baby* for the skin.

So tell your story, find the grace-bearers, receive the *poor babies*, and wrap up in the fuzzy blanket hugs. Sur-thrive.

Katie's Story: A Mama's Love

My sweet mama has devoted herself to walking with us through the difficult days of parenting older adopted children. One night after work, she arrived to pick me up for Bible study. She found me sobbing on the couch in the fetal position, overwhelmed with the trials of the day. She took one look at me, scooped me up, and let me cry. Then she went to my kids and had a little "chat" about how they were to treat her daughter and their mother. She called me into the kitchen, asked if I had eaten, and commanded me to pour myself a glass of wine. When I finished, she escorted me to the car, drove to Bible study, and picked up burgers and fries when it was over. Now that's a mama's love.

—*Katie K.*

Spike the Vampire Dog

In the middle of the in-freakin-fertility, Alex surprised me with a tiny Yorkie. This was the height of self-sacrifice for my pet-averse husband. I named him "Spike" after my favorite vampire from *Buffy the Vampire Slayer*, and I carried him all over DC in a little black purse. Spike has seen more theater than most of my friends. I'll never forget the time he pooped in the middle of the costume shop of The Shakespeare Theatre or the day he started humping his plush toy when I was in the middle of a fitting with an actress.

He was a one-owner dog, and he followed me everywhere. When I was at my lowest, he curled up on the couch with me and let me rub his belly. He was my first child, my furry baby when I couldn't have the human variety. I'm convinced he saved my life when I was so low and didn't know if I'd have the strength to keep living.

Last summer, one month after we finalized Ana's adoption, Spike died. For about a year, his kidneys were in renal failure, but miraculously he showed no signs of slowing down. But as we wrapped up Ana's paperwork and finished the court and embassy trips overseas, Spike finally let go of life and slid away from us, like he knew I would be okay. All my babies were here. Our family was complete. And he could rest.

Via Unexpected.org
July 28, 2014

"Spike," I sobbed, "please don't go. I'm not ready. It's not enough time. Stay. Please stay with me."

Spike looked at me through fading eyes as if to say, "You can do this. You're ready. I've given you everything I have."

I touched his dry, blackened tongue, once soft and bubblegum pink. I placed my hand on his heart, thumping deep in his sunken chest, and I felt it slow and stop beating.

He was gone.

I've talked to so many people who have received comfort from pets during suffering and loss that I'd be remiss not to mention them here. These animals are living fuzzy blankets, and they tend to us in ways that no one else can. I'm a firm believer in the power of fuzz therapy.

Poor baby. Here's a fuzzy blanket. And a puppy. And then we sit together in the tension of the hard questions.

Comfort Foods That Will Help You Eat Your Feelings

Jenny Myer: It's got raisins in it . . . you like raisins.
—*Better Off Dead*[1]

Okay, so we covered some basic coping techniques, like sharing your story, finding the grace-bearers, curling up in a fuzzy blanket, and petting furry puppy bellies. The next coping technique I'm going to mention is so basic, yet so big, that it deserves its own chapter, not to mention its own set of 3 x 5 recipe cards (but don't ask me for any because I'm not that organized). I'm talking food, you guys. Comfort food.

I'm not really a cooker person, and I do struggle with stress non-eating from time to time, so when I'm in a rough place, I just try to eat whatever sounds good. Salads are out. Salads are for people who love their lives enough to stomach a bowl full of garden weeds. These people are bursting with purpose and hope and shiny happy exuberance. They think lettuce makes them feel better.

Salads are not for us. Not now. Not when we're wrapped in our fuzzy blankets binge-watching *Sherlock*. (Could Benedict Cumberbatch be considered a comfort food? No, Melanie, that's so inappropriate. Yes, you're right.) So here are some ridonkulously easy comfort foods that I love. Eat them all by yourself or share them with your family or roommates or reasonably-sized litter of cats.

Sausage and Spinach Gnocchi

This recipe from *Real Simple* magazine is super easy, and yet my family thinks I work so hard to create this awesomeness.[2] My sister-in-law Jennifer made this last year, and it was the greatest thing my taste buds had ever known. And the ingredients list is short, which is a must for me even when life is good, much less when everything is hard.

The recipe calls for two 9-ounce refrigerated packs or one 17.5-ounce shelf-stable pack of gnocchi. I use one 12-ounce shelf-stable box of gluten-free potato gnocchi, and it's so good I moan audibly while biting into its chewy goodness. Whatever you use, cook it how the box tells you to and drain it, save about a quarter cup of the pasta liquid, and leave it all for a sec.

Meanwhile, heat a tablespoon of olive oil in a large pan on medium, add a chopped onion, and cook until it's softened. Add in a pound of Italian sausage. I use mild so my kids don't revolt on me, and I try to buy it loose, but sometimes I have to buy it already stuffed inside the casings and spend an extra couple minutes squirting sausage guts out of the casings into the pan. Whatever. Use your spoon to chop it up with the onions in the pan until it's nice and brown. (By the way, you may notice me referring to actual units of measurement. Please. Do not think for a second that I do anything more than casually eyeball everything and hope for the best.)

Add in a chopped clove of garlic (I Microplane my garlic directly into the pan, which makes me feel all cool, like Rachel Ray.), about five ounces of baby spinach (Is there grown-up spinach? I feel like I never see that.), a dash of salt, a dash of pepper, badabing, badaboom, and toss around until the spinach wilts.

Add in the cooked gnocchi, the pasta liquid, ¾ cup grated Parmesan, and toss it around. You might be fancy with the cheese. I use the kind that comes in the green can. We are not so fancy.

Divide it into bowls, serve the green can alongside so people can sprinkle on extra cheese if they want, and if you're dairy-free, just omit the cheese altogether and it still tastes amazeballs.

Pizza Pasta

I made this up, and you won't be surprised when you see how dumb this is. But my family loves it and I can eat bowls and bowls.

Boil a bag of noodles according to the package directions. I use Trader Joe's brown rice and quinoa gluten-free curly boingy pasta. When I first tried these noodles, I didn't believe they were gluten free and thought for sure TJ's was trying to poison us.

While the noodles are cooking, brown a pound of ground beef, add in chopped pepperoni, then a jar of spaghetti or pizza sauce. Whatever you have, because you are sad and life is hard and let's don't get stupid with the crazy parameters. Let it all bubble.

At this point, if I don't feel like making a separate vegetable, I add in finely chopped spinach so my kids don't know what's happening as I try to make them healthy. Or not. Just whatever.

Drain the noodles, mix the sauce and noodles together. Serve in bowls with optional Parmesan cheese on top.

If you make your own pizza sauce or hand grate your own Parmesan cheese, that's great for you and don't tell me about it. Don't be a hero.

Potato Bar

The potato is God's greatest food invention of all the inventions. When I don't have time to cook a potato all by myself, I grab drive-thru waffle fries. This happens about four times a week.

When I do have time, or at least ten minutes of energy available for food prep, I stab a bag's worth of baking potatoes with a fork. (This is a great activity for the angry days.) Rinse the potatoes, stab repeatedly with a fork, then wrap individually with foil.

Nestle their li'l tushes in a big Crock-Pot and cover and cook on low for eight-ish hours. I say -ish because it depends on the Crock-Pot and how many potatoes, so just use your brain and figure it out, okay? I'm not a cook scientist. You'll work it out.

I create a little toppings bar of cheddar cheese, dairy-free faux cheese, sour cream, butter, faux butter, chopped chives, cooked broccoli, chopped bacon, salt, and pepper. Just whatever you like on a potato. Chili would be yummy. Marshmallows . . . not so much. (When you chop the broccoli, you must sing Dana Carvey's "Choppin' Broccoli" song. You must. It's in the Bible.)

Then I let people go nuts and I mash my own potato with a fork and feel better about my life. And everyone thinks I'm a freaking genius because I put potatoes in a pot and gave them the power of choice.

Bacon-Wrapped Chicken

Growing up, my mom made this recipe, and it's still one of my favorites. Layer a 9 x 13 Pyrex with prosciutto or chipped beef. Some kind of thin-sliced salty meat. Grab a couple pounds of skinless boneless chicken breasts. If they're the hormoned-up, Dolly Parton double-D chicken boobs they sell in the store, cut them in half, cuz we want full bacon-flavor penetration, otherwise you're looking at a boring piece of chicken. Wrap each breast, natural or augmented, in a piece of bacon. I know. We currently have three meats going on in here. I'm excited too. Nestle the bacon breasts in the dish.

> **Via Twitter @UnexpectedMel**
> Eating turkey jerky to avoid another cup of coffee to wake up. It's not working and now I have the meat sweats.
> #amwriting

Mix a can of cream of mushroom soup with a half pint of sour cream. If you're dairy-free-ish like me, stir together a tub of Tofutti sour cream, a cup of unsweetened almond milk, and a dry packet of dairy-free mushroom soup. Dump it all over the breasts.

Bake at 275 degrees for two to three hours.

I cook rice and green beans to go with it because the sauce is awesome and I like to drizzle it on the rice. Feel better. Smoky meat is good.

Guacamole

Guacamole can be considered a whole meal around here. My friend Fabiola's husband, Pavel, makes the best guacamole I've ever had in my life, and I've developed my own extremely lazy version of it that I make weekly. Mine takes four ingredients, so even on the hardest of days, I can manage to eke this one out.

Crush four perfectly ripe avocados into a bowl. Add the juice of two limes (or two avocados and one lime, depending on whether or not you have to share). Sprinkle in dried oregano and garlic salt. That's it. No chopping whatsoever, unless you count slicing open the limes and avocados. Fork mash and stuff your face.

So that's sausage, pasta, potato, bacon, and guac. These are the heroes of comfort food. And if you need chocolate, then I recommend dark chocolate chips right out of the bag. No need to stand on ceremony.

Because Sometimes Suffering Is Funny

> Dr. Pearl: People say, "You must have been the class clown."
> And I say, "No, I wasn't. But I sat next to the class clown, and I
> studied him."
>
> —*Waiting for Guffman*[1]

Using humor to cope with suffering is a time-honored technique. Just look at *Harry Potter and the Prisoner of Azkaban*. Those boggarts didn't stand a chance against the *Riddikulus* spell. In Harry's world, a boggart is a creature that assumes the shape of whatever the person seeing it most fears. To defeat a boggart, you use a *Riddikulus* charm, which involves turning the horrible fear that's tormenting you into something completely absurd. This causes laughter and defuses the boggart's power.[2] The spell might not be real, but levity really is the perfect neutralizer of the pain that holds us prisoner.

For a long time, my boggart was never having a baby, and I would picture Alex and myself as Meryl Streep and Goldie Hawn in *Death Becomes Her*, childless and alone, cackling together in the back of the church at Bruce Willis's funeral. Of course I was Goldie and Alex was Meryl, who looked completely stunning in an evening gown. (Upon reading this, my long-suffering husband asked why he's always a woman in my analogies. For once, can't he be Bruce Willis? I told him I'd take it under advisement and he should feel honored to be Meryl.)

When Alex and I were in the thick of our struggle with infertility, our favorite coping mechanism was humor—a very oddball, totally inappropriate brand of infertility humor. I would joke about being a reproductive disaster, he'd say something about his sperm, and the people around us would back away slowly and set their teeth in a gapless smile so the crazy couple wouldn't bother them. We were self-deprecating and gross, but what might strike outsiders as inappropriate was completely appropriate for us at the time. Humor is how we survived and found fun and found ourselves, our us-ness, in the midst of the hopelessness of our situation.

We're doing the same thing now, in the midst of this current season of diagnoses and treatments, because when you're racing home from the psychiatrist to make it in time for the therapist, you have to laugh. I've taken to stocking Ben and Jerry's "Chocolate Therapy" ice cream in the freezer for the kids on therapy days. Everybody just laugh and eat ice cream. We're all gonna be fine. My kids actually continue to teach me how to laugh through the pain. After one particularly heavy, difficult conversation, I asked if my child wanted me to change the subject, and the answer was a resounding yes, so I pulled out my phone and showed them all a video of a unicorn pooping rainbow ice cream and we died laughing. You can take breaks from working through the hard stuff. Sometimes you need unicorn poop.

The best thing that ever happened to me was when I discovered it was okay to find things funny. I hadn't seen humor modeled in the church. I hadn't seen women being funny. Growing up, guys were funny and women were precious, and Christians were serious as a heart attack. I tried to be serious. Seriously. But that didn't work.

Over time I've learned the value in making light of heavy things. They don't become less important, but Big Scary Monsters lose their power over you when you laugh at them. Laughter makes you stronger.

And sometimes when you're experiencing Big Feels, it's hard to let out one without letting out all of them. When you take the top off the crammed-up bottle your emotions are in, everything sprays out. The anger, the pain, and the humor. And it feels so good to let it all out in one frothy steam.

It's okay to grieve, to feel a loss. And it's okay to be happy and sing at the top of your lungs. And those two things can happen within five minutes of each other. That's what I love about feelings. We get to have whichever ones we feel when we feel them and they can make no sense back-to-back and that's okay.

So let yourself laugh even when you worry you aren't supposed to. Not at someone else's expense, but at your own stuff. You own that, and you can laugh at it if you want to.

Moments of Absurdity

Laughing defuses the power the bad stuff has over your life. Have you noticed this with kids?

When my kids are mad and yelling or talking back to me or generally angsty, I get them to do jumping jacks. They look at me like I'm crazy, but I insist. And as they start swinging their arms and legs akimbo, their frowny faces relax and they start giggling. Every. Single. Time.

Via Twitter @UnexpectedMel

Elliott: Daddy, you're a Storm Pooper.

#SeeWhatHeDidThere

Sometimes when you're in the middle of something hard, you have these moments of absurdity. It's like you pull out of your body and hover above yourself, like an alien coming down to check out the earthlings and learn their ways. And you see yourself and what you're having to do, and it all seems so strange.

During our infertility treatments, Alex and I would drive into DC every morning for me to get poked with needles and examined by ultrasound. In the movies, the ultrasound is on the outside, and it's all very cute, and there's usually a baby in the big shiny tummy, which is tastefully covered by a cloth. In my real life, the ultrasound was a Bilbo-shaped (They aren't going to let me say the shape here, I just know it, so it's kind of like a Hobbit name but not.) wand, the internal kind that went up . . . just . . . up, and we sat in the dark with doctors and ultrasound technicians making comments about my follicles while my precious husband held my pants, and we tried to act like this was totally normal and the way we always pictured getting pregnant.

And so we laughed. A lot. And cried and had huge hormonal swings. (Well, Alex did. I totes held it together like a boss, duh.)

Amy's Story: The Itsy Bitsy Spider

My dad died suddenly of a stroke at age 50. We were all completely shocked and grief-stricken. There we were, sitting at his funeral—me, my hubby, my mom and brother, my dad's younger brothers and his parents—all of us squished together in the front two pews with a room full of the many friends who had come to support us sitting in the rows behind us. Suddenly, in the middle of the service, at which I can only assume was a very serious moment—and I can't remember who noticed it first and pointed it out to all of us fellow family members in the second row—there was a very small SPIDER CRAWLING ON THE PONYTAIL OF BROTHER NUMBER ONE!!!! All of us sitting in that second pew were immediately overwhelmed with waves of trying-to-hold-it-in laughing/crying-uncontrollably fits. I can only imagine what deeply serious thoughts were being spoken by whoever was up front at that time and what the whole room full of people behind us thought of our snickering and snorting at such a deeply grievous event.

—Amy O.

Sometimes laughter in the face of crazy hard awful things is the best and only thing to do. When my grandfather on my mom's side died my senior year of high school, I had to excuse myself to the bathroom . . . to laugh.

Slap-Happy Funeral

I cannot cry at normal times. Instead I will cry over ridiculous things, like the time I broke my neon pink treble clef pen in the car on the way to Atlanta, Georgia, from Cleveland, Ohio, and sobbed hysterically for hours, holding my family hostage to my complete breakdown. I was fourteen and I could tell things weren't going to work out with my boyfriend and the pen was The. Last. Straw.

Crying over ridiculous things comes naturally. Crying at funerals for people I love with all my heart . . . well, I've thought about pulling a nose hair or something to conjure those tears because they aren't happening on their own.

And so at my grandfather's funeral, I found myself in the bathroom stifling guffaws. You see, my mom's side is full of back-slappers. They are a family of back-slapping huggers, and when you get a bunch of them in a room and put them in a situation where there's going to be a lot of comforting and consoling, well, fuhgetaboutit. Commence slapping. So all around the big box where my grandfather lay, the back-slappiest of all, the King of all Back-Slappers, people were hugging and banging on each other's backs. It looked painful. And back-slapping isn't quiet, so all around the room you heard, *Slap-slap-slap, Slap-slap-slap, Slap-slap-slap.* And I could not contain myself, so I ran to the bathroom.

COMFORTING BACK-SLAP

Sometimes you have to latch on to the hilarious in the face of the devastating. Sometimes it's your lifeline.

Letting Yourself Laugh Again

Mining life for the funny moments is kind of similar to keeping a gratitude journal or counting blessings. You hunt for them, actively seek them out.

One of my favorite movies of all time is *Elizabethtown*, which I think nobody really got, but I thought was completely brilliant because it's so absurd that it's real. Orlando Bloom's character had just experienced an epic failure and the death of all his hopes and dreams and in the middle of a suicide attempt, he gets a call that his dad died and he needs to go handle all the arrangements. It's filled with ridiculous characters and family members obsessed with odd details like a blue suit and a cousin with a third nipple, and they argue over burial or cremation.

And in the middle of all the sadness and Orlando Bloom's flat, dead eyes, Kirsten Dunst's character whirls around like a quirky little fairy and teaches him to embrace life. There are these moments throughout when he steps back and finds the absurd humor in the entire situation. I get that. I do that. After his dad dies, his mom goes to comedy school and says, "I figured it out. It takes time to be funny . . . and it takes time to extract joy from life."[3] Yes, it does.

So what are some ways you can cultivate the funny and let yourself laugh again?

Notice the ridiculous. I made jokes about the track marks up my arms from all the needle pokes, and we laughed and I sang eighties tunes at the top of my lungs as Alex gave me butt shots of progesterone every night. He actually drew a smiley face on my butt with the eyes as the injection points. Every time I'd bend over, he'd say, "Smile!" We laughed about hormonally enhanced boobs and how my ovaries were pumped up to the size of grapefruits. And how sexy I felt getting knocked up on a hospital bed with several people in the room with us. I had one procedure done at a teaching hospital, and I think every medical student in the DC-Virginia-Maryland area saw up my gown. Super romantic.

When I was in the hospital for six days after delivering Elliott and my C-section gash wouldn't quit squirting blood and my levels were wonky and everyone was still wondering if I'd stroke out and die, I had to order my loving mom and darling husband out of the room multiple times because they were making me laugh so hard it was hurting my stitches. The hospital was really full, and they kept moving me to a different room. At one point my mom ran out for a second to get food and came back and I was gone. It was like in a movie, where the sheets are folded on the bed and the bad guys got me and I'd been wheeled out and incinerated and there was no record of my ever having been there. After a moment of panic, she hunted around and found where they'd moved me and we got so tickled about the whole thing I had to shove a pillow across my lap to stop the bellyache.

One day no one came to check on me for ages and ages, and my catheter backed up and we were on the brink of a messy pee scenario. They came to empty it, finally, and it resembled that scene from *Austin Powers* when they take him out of cryo freeze and he goes and goes and goes. "Elimination comp—Elimination comp—Elimination complete."[4]

In the middle of the night, Nurse Ratchett ("Call me Bo," she said, in a voice like the imaginary Attila the Hun in my head.) came to take out my catheter and force me out of bed. I stumbled across the floor and barely made it to the toilet before passing out cold and being resuscitated by smelling salts, all while my mom, who really does know best, was saying, "She's not ready. Give her time. Go slowly. She's going to pass out." That whole scenario was worth it for a lifetime of Bo jokes whenever we need a motivational speech. "Don't make me get Bo." Or like the Bo Jackson commercial from my childhood, "Bo knows . . . catheters." "Bo says get up and go." "Call me Bo." "I'm here to get you moving." Over the years our Bo voice has started to sound a lot like Arnold Schwarzenegger.

Surround yourself with funny friends. You know what you need when you need it. You have friends for the crying and you have friends for the laughing. Sometimes you have a rare and beautiful friend who can do both. Don't be afraid to reach out to your funny people and invite them over to make you laugh. And sometimes you need to give the people around you permission to be funny. "Tonight I just want to laugh. No heavy stuff." People will follow your lead, so don't be afraid to tell them what you need. If you don't have funny friends, watch funny movies with your serious friends and hope for the best.

> **Via Twitter @UnexpectedMel**
>
> *My doc: You're gonna poop your brains out.*
>
> *Me: I like a doctor who says "poop your brains out."*
>
> *My doc: It's a technical term.*

Ask funny questions. When my kids are struggling in school, we talk about that, but I also try to ask them questions to get them thinking about other things and grab a peek at the bigger picture. What smelled bad today? Did anything weird happen? Did anyone do something hilarious? What's the craziest thing you learned today from the teacher or from a friend? We can ask ourselves these questions too. What awkward thing happened at work today? Who brought the grossest lunch? When I've had a bad day, sometimes I ask my kids weird questions and just start writing down their answers. And then I tweet them to the universe and take absurd pleasure in it. And then I read them to Alex later and we fall in love with our hilarious kids all over again.

Look at your life as a casual observer. Have an out-of-body experience. If you were watching your life on a movie screen, what would make you laugh if it was happening to someone else? What would you say to Movie Screen You if you were the sidekick giving a pep talk at the schwanky club in the rom-com? What ridiculous nickname would you give the guy who just hurt you, like Mr. Unibrow or Death-by-Khakis? What uber-trendy name would you give your fancy drink in your hipster mason jar? The Crandlebar Mustache (just a splash of cranberry to go with your sneer) or Mumfordtini or . . .

Focus on the moment. Go out to dinner or wherever. Just go.

When you're experiencing whatever you're doing, focus on each moment and keep your thoughts trained on the details right in front of you. The pain will be waiting for you when you're done, but for a moment, for an hour, for a night, focus on joy. Taste the bacon and how it perfectly complements the piece of shrimp it's wrapped around. Inhale the coffee beans. Watch the candle flicker on the table. Let yourself tell a funny story of another time, or laugh as someone else tells a story. If you want to be alone, bring a book, a hilarious memoir or a really fun adventure that sucks you in and engages your imagination.

Hang out with people who have no idea. Exchange silly banter with a waiter. Make small talk with a stranger at a park. Not everyone likes to talk to random people, but sometimes it can feel so good to have a witty conversation with someone who has no idea what you're going through. One time during Infertile Inferno, I went to a salon I'd never been to before and had a guy dye my hair Sydney Bristow red. (This was at the height of *Alias*. You know the red I mean.) I was snarky and we chatted for hours over metal foil things and lots of chemicals that smelled weird. And after it was over, I had manic-panic red hair and strutted around to No Doubt and felt Hella sure I could take on SD-6 with my bare hands.

We still take the bad stuff seriously. We don't sweep it away. But we laugh through it and find the warped humor in the situation.

Sometimes this is impossible. Things are just too horrible.

But sometimes it's not. Sometimes it's perfect.

Don't Make Me Come Over There

Carol: Everything now, it just consumes you.
Daryl: Hey. We ain't ashes.

—The Walking Dead[1]

Okay, there's a time for wearing fuzzy blankets, for consuming carbs and chocolate, for cracking inappropriate jokes—and then there's a time to get junk done. Here's the part of the book where we move forwardish. Things are still bad, wounds are still maybe a little oozy on the edges, but if we're going to learn to love our lives, we might as well get on with it.

If these sentences are hitting you like when your mom used to yank you out of bed for school in the morning, please feel free to go back to the bacon and the coffee and the hair stroking. Take all the time you need.

This chapter is for when you want and need a little motivation. Peppiness is not for every day. Some days peppiness can eat it. But on those days when you're teetering and could go either way, when you feel like you could get out and really grab today by its shiny high-bounce balls . . . or possibly stay in bed forever and think about all the ways you could die underground (so many options; see end of chapter for details), here is your invitation to greet the day:

Hey.

You are so loved. You are a precious little snowflake. Now get the bleep up and turn the TV off.

Seriously, God loves you so, so much, snowflake. It's time to motorvate. Now.

The Creator of the universe made you and thinks you're beautiful. He made you and said you were good (Genesis 1:31). Put some pants on and walk out the door.

All your days were written in his big holy journal before one of them happened (Psalm 139:16). Nothing surprises him. This is true. I, however, would like to be surprised, so let's get up and greet the freaking day, love.

He wastes nothing. That's always so comforting to me. He isn't going to let any of this go to waste. He's working all things together for the good of those who love him. He's working it all out (Romans 8:28). Fer sher. Doesn't feel that way. Doesn't feel good. You know what would feel really good right about now? A shower. Try it.

Even if life's sucky right now. It's sucky right now, but it isn't wasted suckiness, and that's awfully dang comforting if you ask me. Sometimes. Sometimes it's awfully comforting and sometimes it's just awful. You know what isn't awful? Deodorant. Discover it.

You are enough, and you're doing the best you can. You're enough. *You're enough.* God loved you before you even got out of bed this morning. (And if you're still in bed, he loves you snuggled right inside all the covers.)

C'mon. Let's do this together.

No, seriously, get out of bed. Don't make me come over there.

Holly's Story: I Am Not Forgotten

A few weeks after my husband died of a heart attack at the ripe old age of thirty-nine, finances were about as uncertain as they come. His place of employment had been sold a few days prior to his death, so getting one hot cent from anyone was looking doubtful. So, in one little faltering heartbeat, I went from being well taken care of to not knowing how I was going to support my three little kids. I will never, ever, forget the day, while still in the complete fog of losing my husband, that I attempted to use WIC checks. This is what I wrote that day:

As prepared as we thought we were financially for something like this, we never could have foreseen what has happened here with finances. I know I will be fine. However, all of this craziness has led me to sign up with a couple different government programs, hopefully, for the short term. So, today was the first day that I was going to use these special checks for the basics . . . milk, bread, fruit, etc. . . . . I was told upon receiving them that they would be easy to use and that Wal-Mart knows exactly what to do with them. So I carefully chose a Wal-Mart where I would safely see nobody that I knew. I made my list on my phone so I wouldn't have to pull out the WIC folder, and I headed into no-man's land. Within about eight minutes, I saw someone that I knew. "What are you doing on this side of town?" she asked. I blubbered my way through the question. Then she looked in my cart and said, "That is a really interesting collection of things in your cart." I blubbered some more. I just couldn't believe that I was in Wal-Mart trying to use these ridiculous checks that actually ARE very complicated. I couldn't really tell her all I was thinking, because the tears were already itching to spout out. So I gathered my basics and an Etch-a-Sketch and headed to checkout. My pulse was already rising a little. I didn't know exactly how to execute this exchange and neither did the cashier, for crying out loud.

First of all, she forgot to use one of the checks and made me use cash and then couldn't fix it. "Whatever, I just want to get out of here," is what was circling in my head. Then I needed two cartons of a half-dozen eggs. They were out, so I got a dozen. Seemed logical to me, but she was not satisfied with my answer, so she sent someone to the very last aisle, about a quarter of a mile away, to check for the half-dozen egg cartons.

Meanwhile, I was starting to sweat a little. People kept coming to my line, and she kept saying, "I'm having someone check on a WIC item, so you might want to find another line." I wanted to say, "Do you have to keep telling everyone that I'm on WIC?"

Lo and behold, there were not any half-dozen egg cartons, and so we used the dozen carton that I initially picked up. She proceeded checking me out. Oh, wait. She scanned the orange juice. "You can't get pulp-free orange juice with WIC," she said. I told her that isn't what my little pamphlet said. This time I said out loud, "Whatever—I've gotta go. I'll just pay for it." Again, the egg checker came back and she asked him to check on the pulp-free business. This was just getting ridiculous by this point. I was holding up the line again. She kept announcing, "We're having a WIC problem here." Oh, my gosh. I was sweating like a pig now. This was so embarrassing. I considered leaning in, hitting the switch to the checker light, and saying, "Let's just turn this little guy off for now." The answer came back after I'd already paid for it: pulp free is fine. Oh, my lands. I went through all of that and for so little.

I got in the car. I teared up, and then God began repeating, "Holly, you are a daughter of the Lord Most High."

I am not little, I am not forgotten, I am not less. And neither is anyone who is on WIC, or anyone who has lost a spouse, or anyone in any situation. First John 3:1: "See what great love the Father has lavished on us, that we should be called children of God! And that is what we are!" I am a daughter of the Lord Most High!!!!! He sees me. He sees my crazy life. He sees my children. He loves me. He wants the best for me. He is with me. I don't believe this at all times, but God is faithful to remind me when I need reminding.

—Holly A.

Are your feet on the floor? Are you standing? Did you brush your teeth and hair, wash your face, and maybe change out of your jammies? (I mean, only if you're really motivated. Changing into clean jammies is also an option.) I hope by now you're out of bed and ready to face the day. But if not . . . when you just need to wallow, there's this helpful list:

All the Ways You Could Die Underground

- You could be in the basement of a department store when all the mannequins suddenly come to life and attack you, like in the first episode of the *Doctor Who* revival in 2005.
- You could go spelunking and fall into a ravine deep, deep in the center of a mountain.
- Buried alive. Many years ago, buried alive was all the rage in plotlines. I credit Tarantino for burying Uma Thurman alive in *Kill Bill: Volume 2*. Because then Sydney Bristow got buried alive in *Alias*, and they even buried one of the guys on *CSI*. I think that one involved stinging ants. But hey, in all those cases, everyone survived, although they're probably still in counseling to this day.
- Radon. This is a slow death. I grew up in a basement filled with high levels of radon, which we discovered when I was in college and my parents sold the house and had to install a radon-wicking system. So apparently my entire childhood was filled with radon, and I'm still around. At least I've made it to thirty-seven.
- Zombies. There's always the zombies. They seem to hang out in basements and perk up when you accidentally wander down the stairs.
- Vampires. I mean, clearly, these guys like a good crypt and chilling in the subterranean.
- I lived in DC during all the 9/11, anthrax, terrorism scares and lots of people stopped riding the subway. I still rode the subway and spent several moments wondering if they would

be my last. But I like the subway and figure the zombie thing is probably more likely.

Okay, maybe that's enough brainstorming underground death scenarios. After all, my office is in my basement, and probably the only likely scenario is my choking to death on a Nerds Rope late at night all by myself.

Via Twitter @UnexpectedMel

Me: Evie, why are you coloring Doc McStuffins's eyeballs red?

Evie: I'm making her a zombie.

Me: We are so the same.

Living Like a Cadbury Egg

King Arthur: (*after Arthur has cut off both of the Black Knight's arms*) Look, you stupid b****rd, you've got no arms left!

Black Knight: Yes, I have.

King Arthur: Look!

Black Knight: It's just a flesh wound.
                                    —*Monty Python and the Holy Grail*[1]

I'm more of a fair-trade dark chocolate kind of girl, but around Easter time, nothing gets me more excited than when the Cadbury eggs come out in stores. (This is why I describe myself as "dairy-free-ish." Some things are worth intestinal volcano. You know what I'm talking about.) They take me right back to my childhood. Every year, my mom would buy me a four-pack, and when I went to college, she would mail them to me. Now that I have kids, she gives them the Easter treats, and I'm still trying to decide whether or not to forgive her for such a travesty.

I can make a Cadbury egg last for an hour. I lick and lick the top until the chocolate starts to soften. (It's gross, like watching a mangy dog nibble away at a soggy piece of rawhide. I'm never winning any contests for prettiest eater.) And then, after about twenty minutes, I break through to the creamy inside, the gooey fondant stuff. I die. I'm writing this part in February and really hoping they put these out soon, because I don't know how much longer I can last without one.

I think during my hardest years of infertility, I was like a Cadbury egg. On the outside, I was hard and uncrackable. But if you spent time with me, I would start to melt. I wasn't as hard as I first appeared. And on the inside, I stayed soft.

I kept a soft heart through the pain and struggle, but I will tell you, it didn't come naturally. I had to cultivate the softness, tend to it, and keep it away from freezers.

For a time I made baby clothes for friends. But then that got too painful, so I switched to knitting baby blankets. Less likely to imagine tiny arms and legs. I threw baby showers. One time I gave a friend a pedicure when she was overdue and couldn't see her feet and could only fit into flip-flops because they were so swollen.

I prayed for softness. I practiced loving thoughts about my pregnant friends. I stayed gooey on the inside even as my outside hardened a bit in self-preservation.

And sometimes I did skip a baby shower, and there was that three-month period when I avoided church. Self-preservation is okay. Do what you need to do. But stay gooey on the inside. Find a way.

Staying Soft and Gooey

One big way we stay soft on the inside is through service. When we serve other people, something amazing happens in our hearts. We get humble, we extend a hand to someone who needs something just like we need something, and we feel grateful that we can help.

When I'm struggling with my own life, I never, ever want to serve. I look for ways to get out of it, to justify not serving, and, let's face it, there are always excuses. Aren't there? *Aren't there?* (Imagine me staring you down with overly intense eye contact. Yeah, you see me.)

Via Facebook @UnexpectedMel

Me: Kids, here's a chore.

Ana: NOT FAIR NOT FAIR NOT FAIR.

Me: You're right. It's not fair for an 11yo and a 5yo to do the same amount. Here's an extra chore. Thanks for bringing that to my attention.

Ana: What.

So sign up to go serve somewhere, put it on the calendar in permanent marker, and show up. Even if your mind is still home playing Minecraft on the couch, your hands are sorting canned goods. After a few minutes, you'll get into it and feel good about helping other people. (I'll talk about a big, big way I've experienced this helping other people helping myself thing in chapter 21. I know. Timey whimey. I'm doing the best I can. You can always make this a *Choose Your Own Adventure* novel and flip ahead. But if you do, don't let your future self see you or, you know, ripping a hole in the space-time continuum, time unraveling, the works.)

Another way is prayer. Ask God to soften your heart, cling to his Word, read it out loud. Sometimes I praise him when I actually feel the opposite. I say it out loud, "You are good. You are faithful. You are never failing. Help me to believe that again." Open your mouth and form the words even if your heart doesn't believe it. Let your body do the work and your heart will follow . . . or not. There's something to be said for going through the motions. Feelings aren't everything. And if you just can't praise him because you feel like it would be lying, then say that. "God, I can't praise you because I feel like I'd be lying. I don't feel like you're praiseworthy right now." Say something. When my husband and I have a fight, I don't want to talk to him, but I open my mouth. We might never get to where we totally agree on something, but we speak words and process through until we're in relationship again. And when I'm too mad to speak, I make him a sandwich. I make my hands work even when the words won't come.

I can't make my feelings change, but I can move my body into a place where my feelings can respond. I can't make myself be happy, but I can walk outside and feel the sun on my face. I can't make myself feel generous toward a friend, but I can bake a batch of muffins and take them to her. I can't make myself accept my circumstances, but I can be completely honest with God about how upset I am and put it back on him to change my heart. He's God. Let him do the work in you. All you have to do is show up and talk to him. You don't have to change your mind. You can just plug in and listen to what he has to say.

I always think if I can get my body somewhere, it's a start. If I can move my body or open my mouth, I can let God do the rest.

Via Unexpected.org
June 2, 2011

I was struggling with feeling insignificant today. What do I do? Does what I do really matter? My least favorite question is "What's new with you?" The tires of my brain spin in the mud of my sluggish thoughts, and I come up empty. What's new? What's new? Laundry, cooking, board games, building "caves" out of blankets and pillows, straightening the same room in the house over and over, and oh, yeah, still waiting to finalize my daughter's adoption. It feels like nothing I do really matters. I feel like I need to hop the next flight to Ethiopia or write a book or sell everything or adopt the sibling group of four that I just read about and really, really wish I could adopt.

In desperation, I asked Elliott if he wanted to go to the dollar store and buy sand toys for the beach. It wouldn't be significant, but I'd have stuff in plastic bags to show that I accomplished something for the day. But he said, "No, thank you. I want you to please stay here and keep me comforny." It's his way of saying "company." I love that it's a combination of "company" and "comfortable." Like he's comforted by and comfortable with my company. At first I was incredulous that my son did not, in fact, want to go buy more STUFF. He always wants to buy more stuff, and I rarely let him. But then, I was convicted by the simplicity of his need—my company. That's my significance. To provide company for my sweet boy while he's building a cave of throw pillows and couch cushions. I feel boring whenever I talk to someone who isn't in this same stage of life. But today Elliott reminded me that I'm not boring to him. And after all, what matters more than that?

We find a way to stay soft on the inside even when our outsides get a little harder, we get our bodies in position to serve and pray even when our feelings aren't there yet, and then we count the wins, one by one. Here we go.

Count the Wins (Even While You're Losing)

Gail: John, a change of pace could not come soon enough here for the Barden Bellas. This is not a great way to start their season.

John: Yeah, this number is like an elephant dart to the public's face.

—*Pitch Perfect*[1]

Impossibly, improbably, in the middle of Infertile Hell, my husband planned a trip to New York City for my birthday. We went and saw *The Lion King* on Broadway and ate dinner in the Rainbow Room overlooking the Empire State Building, and I bought fabric in the fashion district, and we rode a carriage through Central Park. I felt like a princess, if princesses have needle marks up and down their arms and hormonally induced Swollen Boobs of Fury. (Seriously, when your ladybags look like a roided-out Bane from DC Comics, it might be time for mama to lay off the sauce.) And I also had an absolutely horrific allergic reaction to one of the fertility drugs I was on, but despite calls to the doctor and feeling like my delicate nether region was a raging inferno, we were in Manhattan and we were eating bagels and remembering that we liked each other and making memories that I still treasure.

We got home and promptly

found out that our intrauterine insemination (IUI) had failed miserably, but hey, WE STILL HAD NEW YORK, and it was this sparkling weekend adventure that reminded me what was important at a time when everything else felt upside down. We didn't wait. We did it when it wasn't perfect—crazy drugs and failed pregnancy and all.

Wait. More Waiting?

Once we moved past the pain and suffering of infertility and entered the world of adoption, we naively thought that since adoption was clearly God's plan for us, it would be easy. It completely was. Except the opposite. This time, instead of personal feelings of injustice ("It's not fair I'm infertile!!!"), I was keenly aware of the unfairness of a little girl waiting in an orphanage, and the thousands of orphans just like her ("It's not fair they don't have families!!!"). In both scenarios, I had zero control over how long the wait would last and what the outcome would be. The big change was the epicenter of the waiting. While in Infertile Hell, the drama was happening inside my body (and dangling off my chest), and in Adoption Hell, everything was happening far away from me, out of sight.

Waiting can be like a ride at Universal Studios, where you stand in line for an hour and see the door up ahead. You finally make it to the door and think, "This is it," only to discover that it just leads you into another room filled with more lines. Life can feel like one holding tank after another.

Are you waiting for a degree or a job or a spouse or a child or a cure? Waiting is the worst. When I was dealing with infertility, every day felt like forever. I lived month by month. When I was shooting up with some new drug or having an ultrasound shoved up my yam or asking the doctors hundreds of questions or enjoying the thrill of a nurse plunging a needle into my vein again and again, I was okay. Those parts were better because I felt proactive. I was doing my part, accomplishing the thing, making it happen.

But the in-between parts—waiting for the time for more testing, waiting to see if all of it worked—that was pure torture. I drove myself mad with the not knowing.

Same with our adoptions. When I was in full-on paperwork mode, I was a fingerprinting, notarizing, apostilling fiend. I felt in charge. I mean, as in charge as you can feel during these things. But once that stack of papers shipped off to other hands, all we could do was wait—on social workers and lawyers and courts.

The waiting can make you feel like you want to chew your own arm off. Waiting for results, waiting for people, waiting for the phone call.

Via Unexpected.org
November 5, 2009

Elliott's favorite thing in the world is apple juice. He calls it "ackle juice." When he asks for it, I'm usually happy to oblige, but the process takes too long for his little two-year-old patience. I get out the sippy cup. He says, "Ackle juice!" I snap in the little plastic spill-proof thingy. He yells, "Ackle juice!" I get the juice out of the fridge. He starts stamping his feet. "Ackle juice!" I pour the cup one-third full. He starts crying and screaming, "Ackle juice!" I fill the rest of the cup with water. "Ackle juice! Ackle juice!!" I screw on the lid. "Ackle juice! Ackle juuuuuuuuice!!!!" By this point, he's worked himself into a frenzy. I don't even want to give him the dang juice anymore and start contemplating how I can discipline a little patience into his heart. He wants the juice, I want to give it to him, but he cannot handle waiting for me to do it my way.

Um, yeah. I think that's how I am with God. What I want more than anything right now is the baby that we're adopting, whoever he or she is. But there's a process that I have to go through. I'm screaming, "Baby! Baby baby babyyyyyy!!!!!"

And crying and stamping my feet. And God's got a process. I've got to wait on him. Because a sippy cup with no lid isn't going to work for a two-year-old boy. And an adoption without the necessary steps isn't going to work for me.

God, give me patience. I thought that I learned this lesson. I keep thinking that I learned this lesson. I haven't learned it. Help me walk this walk, wait this wait, and discover anew a life that is completely dependent on you.

Iffing My Life Away

I wasted pretty much my whole twenties longing for the next stage. It's my biggest regret, of all the regrets. That and when I tried to get the Meg Ryan haircut. (You know the one? Cute, choppy pixie cut?) I ended up looking like my elementary school PE teacher, who used to dance around the gym to "Mony Mony" with her feathered bob blowing in the breeze of her enthusiasm.

I stopped reading my college magazine. I dreaded its fancy cover arriving in my mailbox to tell me about the successes of my classmates. How sad to peak in college when I received my *summa cum laude* degree bedecked in golden tassels of accomplishment. A fat lot of good it had done.

What had I done of consequence during my twenties? I phased down my job as I ramped up the fertility treatments and had nada to show for it—no job, no baby. I was a human incubator with no incubatee inside.

If only I could get pregnant . . . If only I could keep this baby . . . If only the adoption would go through . . . I've spent years, maybe a whole decade, iffing my life away.

What I've learned is to flip my whole perspective and exchange the *ifs* for the *nows*. As you've probably been told bajillions of times, life is about the bleeping journey, and if we *if* it away, we miss it.

So even now, in the waiting, in the sucking, in the agony of open wounds and unmet expectations and unfulfilled dreams, how do you find joy? How do you savor the smell of a rose even as its thorns bite your flesh?

You count and catalog the gratitude, hunt it down, capture and write it and collage it on a wall. You aggressively seek the good amidst the bad and give thanks, give it as an act of defiance against circumstances

seeking your demise. Speak the words, and don't worry if your heart takes a while to catch up. *Thank you* for the coffee. *Thank you* for the heat in the car warming your icy fingers.

You watch a movie and let yourself laugh. Something absurd, something ridiculous, and you let your muscles remember laughter.

And you eat a meal with a friend. Your safe person. If you don't have one, set a place across from yours at the table and ask God to fill it. Pray a brave prayer for future friendship and pay attention for someone in your life to move toward you. You eat a meal with someone and you savor the moments of camaraderie. And it might be exhausting to do it often, so maybe just once, just on occasion, you let yourself feel connected to someone over food.

My friend Fabiola gave such great advice one time when one of our adoptions was falling through, and we were spinning and reeling and trying to figure out what to do. She said to use the scented lotion in the bottom drawer. The special yummy lotion that someone gives as a gift that's too nice and you don't want to waste it on the everyday. Use it. Pull it out of the drawer and put it on your counter and use it now, in the pit.

Light the candle that's huge and expensive that you don't want to waste. You aren't wasting it if it's making your life brighter during a dark time. Buy a cake just because life is worth celebrating. Go out and take a night off from talking about The Thing.

Be gloriously and ridiculously yourself. Dare to hope in the present, in all its squishy mess. Incomplete and messy with lots of question marks.

You write down what you know. You write down what you don't know. You pay attention and record these feelings, because so often we wait for everything to be better before we make a record. We fill a baby book or a wedding album or a vacation scrapbook, but these are the moments, this is the life, your now life, and you are living it and it's worthy of a book all its own. As Mr. Leezak says in *Just Married*, "You never see the hard days in a photo album . . . but those are the ones that get you from one happy snapshot to the next."[2]

No need to wait for the perfect memories. These are the memories you have right now, and they are worthy and lovely even in their painfulness and horribleness. Don't wait to start living until everything is okay and you're a real boy, Pinocchio. Live now as a creaky wooden doll person.

Via Facebook @UnexpectedMel

Me: You guys have to get up early for school.

Kids: That means YOU have to get up early too.

[Pause]

Me: You know what? It's okay to just not go to school. Just be dumb.

Kids: Yes! Let's be dumb!

During Evie's adoption, after several major nail-biting delays, our case finally made it to the top of the pile only to have a translation issue with our marriage certificate shove us back under the pile. They thought it was a document showing that we weren't married because someone translated "abstract" as "absent." Oops. It cost our daughter many more months in a group home.

I was supposed to lead a team to Uganda, and we had no idea when everything would be sorted out in Ethiopia. To stay, to go, how would this all play out? I went forward with the trip, which had a layover in Ethiopia. I sat in the terminal in Addis Ababa knowing that our girl was a few minutes away but unable to do anything about it.

I'm so glad I went ahead and took the team to Uganda because that catapulted me into a long-term, transformative ministry with a group called HopeChest (more on that later). I could've canceled the trip. I could've said, "This is bad timing because we're waiting for our life to begin." I'm so glad I didn't. I got home and two weeks later, I was packing to head back to Ethiopia, this time to step out of the airport and into my daughter's life. In one month, I had two trips to Africa and started two big journeys: one into the world of adoption and another into the world of overseas ministry.

So maybe as you're dealing with a big bad, maybe there's something you should just do anyway even if the timing stinks and you don't know what tomorrow will hold. Maybe you need to grab a night at the improv theater or serve at the food bank or invite the friend over right in the middle of the mess. Or crack open the yummy lotion. Discover the gooey center of a life still baking in the oven.

Whole Moments of Joy

When Evie's nanny pried her away from the comfort of the familiar and placed her terrified body in my arms, I felt her heart break. I felt it because my heart broke with hers. In that moment, as she sobbed and stretched for culture, for race, for known, and was left with me, strange, white, American, we broke together. I rocked her and softly sang Matt Redman's "You Never Let Go" as I wondered how could her heart survive, and how could I be a part of her healing?

Every day we fought for eye contact, for the exhale, for the promise of safety and that it would be okay. At night, Alex and I would look into each other's eyes, exhausted, shattered, broken for our girl, and we'd let out a collective sigh. We'd let all the fear and anger—at the difficulty of the situation, at the loss for our daughter—expel out and we'd say, "Okay. What are the wins?" What were the wins for that day?

It would be that she ate a bowl of oatmeal and seemed to like it.

She made eye contact when I changed her diaper. She liked being outside and feeling the cool air of the rainy season on her skin. She held my hand. These were "wins" in the middle of so much loss for her. She giggled over balloons. She raced around the house in the middle of a balloon ball and shrieked with happy laughter. She tossed rice in the air and happily smeared it on her face. She stacked Legos into a tower and knocked it down. She reached her arms up for a hug. Wins. We noted each one. I wrote them down. I held onto them for her.

Via Twitter @UnexpectedMel

Evie: Look, Mom, I can put your earplugs in my ears.

Me: Absolutely not. These are a personal item. Never put something in your body that's been inside somebody else's body. That's just a good rule of thumb.

It's been four years since we counted the wins for our brave, strong, brilliant little girl. These days all five of us are processing our pasts and our futures. The wait for each other is over, and this new work of family has commenced. We're each scarred and scared and gifted and graced in our own ways. And we count the wins together.

Are you waiting for healing? For a next step? It's agony, isn't it? Every single day, fight to find the wins. Search them out amidst the nothingness. Where are the wins?

I spent twelve years building my family, and each day felt like an eternity as the clock ticked and the needles stabbed and the paperwork expired. And now that we're together, we count the wins of healing and coping. Whatever you're waiting on, however long you've been waiting, count the wins. Find the moments to savor, when the longing falls away and it's just you with the wind against your skin. A steaming cup of coffee. The sparkling eyes of a stranger who smiles at you.

There's the pain of waiting and there's the pain of enduring, for some things have no end. You wait and wait and that is nearly unbearable, but the enduring . . . that takes practice, getting up every day knowing that this, too, will be hard. Both in the waiting and in the enduring, you have to find joy. And for the enduring, especially, because there is no green pasture on the other side, only the joy to be dug up in your own yard.

The longing is always there, like the pain in my ovary, but counting the wins reminds us of the beauty in the journey toward wholeness. We may never find wholeness this side of heaven, but we may find whole moments of joy.

Hell Is Other People . . . Or Is It Heaven?

What to Do When Other People Make It Worse . . . and How Other People Can Make It Better

Things You Should Say If You Want a Good Face Punch

So you're going through something crazy hard, and to make things even worse, the people around you are . . . well . . . bless their hearts. (I learned this one from my Southern friends, and at first it weirded me out and now I love it. It's like charming, Southern, socially acceptable sarcasm. It means, "What a bleeping idiot.") They mean well. But sometimes the things they say. And sometimes the things I've accidentally said. Sometimes people, including us, are just morons.

So in this chapter let's manhandle all kinds of Christian go-to phrases for the suffering soul, like our favorites, "God never gives you more than you can handle," and "Let go, and let God," and "God's timing is perfect." C'mon, it'll be fun. The basic conclusion: Just don't go there. Just *shhh*. Don't be a moron.

"God never gives you more than you can handle." This little nugget of poo has been plopped onto our plates for consumption, and I'd like to flush it down the toilet where it belongs. He does give us more than we can handle. He absolutely does. Actually, in this misappropriated verse (1 Corinthians 10:13), Paul was talking about temptation, not suffering. When people tell you that, meaning that you must be able to handle a lot or to make you feel better, like God believes that you can handle it, it's completely acceptable to have flames shoot directly out your eyeballs and incinerate them on the spot, like Cyclops in *X-Men* when he takes off his glasses. Oh, yeah, you are so darn strong and can clearly handle the blubbery blue whale on your shoulders right now. Because you're strong! And can handle it! And you can obviously handle it more than the person next to you, who seems to have nary a wrinkle in her life. Yay for handling it!

Even God gave Jesus more than he could humanly handle, and even Jesus moaned, "My Father, if it is possible, may this cup be taken from me" (Matthew 26:39). But did God rescue him from mocking and whipping and searing pain? No, he did not.

Via Twitter @UnexpectedMel

Our road trip:

I'm bored I'm bored I'm bored I'm bored AHHHHH WHO FARTED WE'RE GONNA DIE!!! . . . I'm bored I'm bored are we there yet?

So we end up with more than we can handle. Way more sometimes. And if God is God and could've done it differently but didn't, what do we do with that? On top of the pain from the utter lack of fairness and the total life fail, you also have to admit that you're a little mad at God, which leaves you feeling uncomfortable. It was easier when you liked him and trusted him completely. What do you do with a God you aren't sure you trust anymore? (Isn't it fun having this internal theological brain-melt in the middle of talking to someone? This is why God invented Toblerone.)

"Let go, and let God." No, she didn't. No, she did not just say that to you. Because that's why you still haven't met The One or had The Baby or found peace about The Thing. It's because you haven't let go. You should've let go, dummy, and then all your problems would be solved. God's standing right there waiting for you to let go, but he can't do anything. He's stuck on the sidelines, completely powerless to fix things, while you white-knuckle your life. But of course, as soon as you let go, everything will be perfect. Whew, thank goodness your sweet friend here was there with that sage advice. (Even if you come to the conclusion that you need to let something go, you probably don't want random people telling you this. And if they sing it like Elsa, they are dead to you. So dead.)

"God's timing is perfect." I can't even. I am can't-evening so hard over here. Surrriously. Some people need a mute button. God's timing is perfect, but you know what isn't? Someone saying this to you. Ever. H to the no. Unless you're enjoying a congratulatory toast to something awesome happening, in which case, clink the glasses and celebrate the glorious timing. But when you are hurting, when you are waiting, you do not want to hear that this agony is anything close to perfection. It's not perfect. It's perfectly horrible. Your friend's humanity should tell him, "Hmm, maybe that's not the best thing to say right now or maybe ever."

"Do you have any unconfessed sin that's causing this?" Who are these people talking to you? Oh, my word. C'mere, you need a hug. These are the same friends who talked to Job in the Old Testament and to the blind man in the New Testament. Jesus answered them when he said it was neither this man's sin nor his parents' but so that God's glory could be displayed (John 9:2–3). And that's the truth. Sometimes bad things happen not because we've sinned but because it's life in a fallen world. (Sometimes consequences happen because we've sinned, obviously, but this is not that.) (Just to be clear, friends, say nothing about God's glory being on display while your friend is in the fetal position on the floor with weeping and gnashing of teeth. You know this. You would never.)

Handling the Well-Meanies

So besides face punching, which is tempting, how do we handle the people who mean well, the well-meanies? First, there are going to be times when you just need to avoid them. And that's okay. Like I said before, I had to miss church for a few months during the height of my struggle with infertility. I loved church, and no one was awful, but I needed a break from everyone and

PLATITOOD LIBS

God won't give you more
than you can _____.
                 verb
Just let go and let _____.
                 proper noun
You just have to have
_____. It was _____
noun   verb
to be. Everything
_____ for a reason.
  verb
This is God's _____.
                noun
_____ heals all wounds.
noun
The _____ Dance
     famous egg
is your chance, so do
the _____.
   synonym for wednesday

the questions and the pregnant bellies. It wasn't forever, but it was a season. And I had to say no to a couple of baby showers. Sometimes you need to stay home and heal. Choose your inner circle wisely. Give yourself the power to be your own boss and set your own limits. You don't owe anyone answers or smiles.

Second, I like a little gentle sarcasm. I don't mean being harsh, because most of these people are friends and loved ones. I mean if you're confronted by a friend who makes an inappropriate comment, you can choose to make light of it while gently showing them that maybe that's not the best thing to say. Remember to smile and chuckle and avoid overly intense eye contact.

Them: God never gives you more than you can handle.
You: Then clearly I'm the strongest and best person here.
    I am absolutely amazing. He obviously thinks I'm
    incredible. I hope I win an award for how incredible I am.
Them: Let go, and let God.
You: Well, I did let go, but I ended up with two broken legs
    at the bottom of a cliff.
Them: God's timing is perfect.
You: That's so true, because this feels perfect. Really
    perfect. I can't think of a better schedule than what we
    have right here.
Them: Do you have any unconfessed sin that's causing this?
You: Wait, you mean, like, because I've held a guy hostage
    in the trunk of my car for the last week or maybe on
    account of my raging meth addiction?

However, if you're paralyzed with an inability to confront, revert to Strategy #1: Avoidance. Pretend like you didn't hear them. Pretend like you didn't see them. Pretend like you're seeing psychedelic rabbits.

So, avoidance, sarcasm, and then the third option is a solid smoldering stare. When you can't avoid them and the words escape you, the smoldering stare is your best friend. Maintain eye contact, and if you have the muscular control, raise an eyebrow.

"You Just Have to Have Faith" and Other Stupid Mouth Sounds

"You just have to have faith." "Pray harder." "Fast more self-lessly." "Wait on God more patiently." I had big gold stars by all the Christian categories of waiting, and my uterus was still a barren wasteland. I was the man by the pool waiting for a miracle, and day after day, my miracle didn't come. What do you do when faith "fails"?

If you've ever gone through a difficult time, you've probably encountered those helpful people who feel obligated to give you a pep talk. Like coaches in a locker room during halftime, they come up to you at church or sideswipe you in the grocery store, tilt their heads to the side, and ask, "How's it going?" If you haven't gotten pregnant, beaten cancer, "gotten over" the ginormous hole in your heart, or whatever it is you're supposed to be working on and checking off the list, they give you the Pity Face (more on that later) and proceed to Matt Foley you, with a van down by the river. Their motivational speeches vary depending on your circumstances, but I've encountered a couple of different versions.

In Version One, the person with Pity Face checks to make sure you're doing the steps. Are you using the right essential oils, cutting out gluten, going to the chiropractor, and keeping a journal of your feelings? And it's still not better? Then they prescribe new coping strategies. Try this doctor that did wonders for her sister, electroshock therapy, leeches.

In Version Two, Pity Face person sees you as a flight risk to the faith. Your faith is failing. That's the problem! You just need to have more faith. More faith will fix everything. Because if you're still sad about something and having emotions toward God about it, then you must be lacking in the faith department. Pity Face begins a rousing motivational speech about faith, reminds you of why God is real, and probably cites Hebrews 11.

This happened to me a lot. I expressed negative emotion about being infertile, and well-intentioned people would mistake that for not believing in God. Look, I believed in God, I never stopped believing that he was real. I even believed he had a plan. I just didn't like his plan. And I thought that was okay to communicate. I still do.

We see throughout the Bible plenty of people not liking God's plan. As I already pointed out, even Jesus said, "Lord, if you are willing, take this cup from me," followed by, "yet not my will, but yours be done" (Luke 22:42). There's the tricky part. Not my will but yours. Ugh. That's hard, especially when it feels like the total opposite of what you want.

CUSTOMER SURVEY

1. How satisfied are you with God's plan?
   - ☐ fully satisfied
   - ☐ somewhat satisfied
   - ☐ #!@?%

2. How likely are you to request his services again?
   - ☐ highly likely
   - ☐ possibly
   - ☐ if I'm falling out of a helicopter

3. Will you recommend him to a friend?
   - ☐ definitely
   - ☐ maybe
   - ☐ to a frenemy

I felt like I'd done everything right. My entire life, if I worked hard and tried my best, I usually achieved what I wanted. Good grades. A college I loved. A job that . . . wasn't completely horrendous. And then infertility hit, and there was nothing I could do to get what I wanted. I couldn't meet with a teacher, I couldn't do an interview, and I couldn't study hard for an embryo. I prayed, I fasted, I read the Bible, I dug into my faith and did all the steps I'd been taught, but I could not find the magic combination of faith and works that would unlock my uterus. After a lifetime of overachieving and checking boxes in Christianity, it felt like faith failed. My faith in God didn't really fail, but it felt like my faith failed me. Which was disconcerting. Why wasn't God listening?

Have you ever felt like that?

> **Via Twitter @UnexpectedMel**
> *Kids: *fight grumble argue**
> *Alex: I declare a quiet car until we get home.*
> *Kids: *tattle whine**
> *Me: Unless you're bleeding or swallowed your own tongue, we don't want to hear about it.*

The Difference Between Faith and Sounding Like an Automaton Droid

When you're stuck in the middle of something crazy hard and people are asking how you're doing, there's so much pressure to respond well, like you owe everybody perfect answers. It makes me grumpy. And if you add in faith, then there's added pressure to respond like a happy human being AND a faithful believer. You have to beam out your Care Bear Stare while simultaneously rocking out to the power ballad "Don't Stop Believin'." It's exhausting. And most of the time, it's all lies and what you really want to tell people is you ate gummy worms for breakfast and you stayed in your bathrobe for five days straight and you haven't shaved in a month. And you have no idea if you'll dig out, and you have no idea what God's thinking, and you have no idea how to have real conversations and behave like a regular person anymore.

And so we act like droids, and not even quirky ones like C-3PO. We smear smiles on our faces and answer questions with, "God's got this. I know everything will work out for the best. I'm believing."

Once more with feeling.

Sometimes my robot smile hurts.

So there's droid you, and then there's Dark Side of the Force you, when you want to smash a chair against a wall for dramatic flair and wave your fist in the air and say, "How am I doing? How am I doing? I'm great. So fantastic. (Smash chair.) How are you?" (Rip ice cream cone out of their hands and smush it on the table and quote Happy Gilmore's line, "The price is wrong, b****."[2])

And then there's you you, not Stepford Droid, not Hulk Smash, but the you in the middle. And someone wants to know how you're doing. And they aren't awful (probably). They care (probably). And you respond.

"I know this is kind of cheesy and lame, but I wrote about it on my blog/Facebook/CaringBridge because I don't have the emotional capacity to answer a lot of questions right now. But the fact that you asked means the world to me, and I would absolutely love for you to stop by my little spot on the Internet."

"I am hanging in there." (Hanging in there is always acceptable. It's the vanilla of answers. It's boring, slightly more indicative of struggle than "I'm fine" but reveals nothing. Use liberally as needed, with or without head tilt or shoulder shrug.)

In my head when I hear all the sayings, I think, "Die, perky person, die," with *Psycho re-re-re-re* stabbing sounds from the shower scene. Sometimes when you're hurting, the last thing you want is a perky person trying to cheer you up. They say things like "At least you had some good times together," and "It's not all bad." Sometimes it feels all bad and sometimes you fantasize flicking them right in the middle of the face.

Sometimes we need to stop trying to make each other feel better and just be together. Just join our friends in their ashes and sit quietly by their side.

Laura and Kate's Story: Care for Some Company?

Entering into another's suffering is a choice—it is intentional, purposeful, and results in its own form of suffering. My best friend's suffering became my own when I chose to bear it with her.

The decision to enter into my friend's sufferings was more than caring about her troubles, desiring to serve her, or even genuinely being upset/saddened/angered over her plight. It was a combination of those things, but it was so much more. It was a choice, driven by love, to intentionally and consistently walk with her through the highs and the lows of her situation. It was a determination to selflessly love with compassion, understanding, and gentleness . . . and to establish a presence in the suffering.

It was as if my friend had fallen into a septic tank. Not just knee deep . . . all the way in. At times, the crap was over her head. There were several ways to respond to and interact with her (and her mess):

> Friend 1: "Ew."
>
> Friend 2: (with megaphone, from far away) "How are you doing?"
>
> Friend 3: (wearing face mask) "That looks awful. I'm sorry you fell in there. Maybe I could bring you a meal sometime."
>
> Friend 4: (approaches the edge of the septic tank) "I heard you fell in crap and I wanted to come see you. I thought you might be hungry, so I brought you dinner and some air freshener."
>
> Friend 5: "I'd like to be in there with you. Care for some company?"

I remember telling her: "I don't want to just serve you and cook you meals and do that stuff—that's fine and all—but I want to be with you."

The intentionality of entering into her sufferings proved to be far more painful than I ever could have anticipated. Watching a sweet baby boy die of cancer is agonizing, and there is an even more severe pain in watching my beloved best friend lose her son. Yet we have found beauty in the brokenness.

This same suffering that has caused unimaginable heartache is also rich soil in which our friendship has been cultivated. The soil of suffering and its painful growing conditions yield deep roots and beautiful fruit: great comfort, transparency, heart healing, profound joy.

—*Laura F. and Kate R.*

The Breath Before the Answer

But why, you might ask, why on earth do Christians say these things to one another? Why do we do it? Our unfortunate circumstances trigger others' fears that the vending machine God on TV, the one where you stick in your prayers and out pops health, wealth, and happiness, is all a big sham, like those arcade games where you try to get the claw to pick up a cheap plush toy. *What do you mean God doesn't always answer prayer? The Bible says the Bible says the Bible says the Bible says.*

The Bible isn't a Magic 8 ball that you shake, and it isn't Google where you look stuff up and it gives you exact, step-by-step instructions. Our lives are nuanced and unique. There is no script with lines and stage directions to follow to the letter.

Christians want our faith to be if/then, because the alternative is so much harder. We shy away from tension, but that's where real faith is forged, in the tension. Sometimes our faith is fine, our prayers are happening, we're checking all the boxes, and God says, "No," "Wait," or worse . . . nothing.

Don't be too quick to resolve the tension. And definitely don't let the people around you try to resolve it for you. Sometimes there's a big inhale before God speaks. We need to spend more time in the breath before the answer. That breath can last a lifetime.

Faking Healthy and the "I'm Fine" Smile

> Buffy: I've been making shows of trading blows
> Just hoping no one knows
> That I've been going through the motions
> Walking through the part
> Nothing seems to penetrate my heart.
> —*Buffy the Vampire Slayer*[1]

We have this uncanny ability to live beneath a façade of normality while inside so many of us are dying a little. After Elliott was born, Alex and I looked like a cute family with our beautiful, blond-haired, blue-eyed, dimpled baby boy, but whenever anyone asked when we were going to have more kids, I'd have to super-glue the cracks in the façade. I wanted to scream, "I'm not fine!" When you're ready to freak out in the church lobby, this chapter is for you.

My parents and I DVR *The Tonight Show*, then text about it while we watch from our respective houses. And Mom worries.

> Mom: I'm worried about Jimmy.
> Me: Jimmy who?
> Mom: Fallon.
> Me: I think he's doing okay.
> Mom: When he introduced The Roots the other night, he
>   didn't seem as energetic as usual.
> Me: Really? I didn't notice.
> Mom: Usually he's like, "Give it up for THE ROOTS!"

and yesterday he just said, "Give it up for The Roots." I think he's tired.

Me: Well, he and Nancy just had a baby.

I still think Jimmy is probably fine and just happened to choose a different inflection one night, but this kind of thing happens to us all the time. If we aren't on at all times, friends start to worry we aren't perky enough and try to re-perk us.

People in general, and maybe Christians in particular, are highly gifted spies capable of layers of subterfuge when it comes to how we're really feeling. The church lobby could be the perfect setting for a James Bond spy movie. All it's missing is a really sultry tango. But what it lacks in tango and roses between the teeth, it makes up in handshaking greeters and those tiny communion cups.

Life could be blowing up like the Clean Slate protocol in *Iron Man 3*, but you walk through those church doors and you are *on*. "How are you?" "I'm fine." Really? "Really, just so blessed. The Lord is good. We are so, so, so blessed. Hashtag blessed."

These Routine Questions

People would ask me all the time, "So when are you going to have more kids?" And the dreaded "How are you doing?" (Of course, featuring Pity Face. I'll unpack Pity Face in just a second.)

I had many different answers. Here were some:

- Stone face silence. Just stare them down. Don't flinch and don't let yourself smile. They'll eventually say, "That bad, huh?" and walk away or burst into tears and walk away. The important thing is away. Away with you, awkward question asker. We'll have none of that around here.
- Launch into a long explanation about my period and ovulating and how my fallopian tube hurts. Use words like "discharge" and "endometrial lining."
- Yell, "NOW!" really loudly. "We're going to have more kids NOW!" "We're going to get over the painful loss NOW!"

We're going to whatever-they-think we-should-do "NOW!" Run away screaming "NOW!" And wave your hand in the air like you're riding the bull.

- "How am I doing? How am I doing? Well, my allotted grieving time is over, so of course I'm fine. These things usually really only take a week. The death of a dream only takes, phew, yeah, just about a week to get over. So I'm great. Fandiddlitastic." (Okay, honestly, some of these I only ever did in my head. I'm kind of regretting that now. But I do like still having friends.)

Via Twitter @UnexpectedMel

Me: When you start puberty . . . b/c puberty . . . then w/the puberty . . .

Ana: Agh!

Me: Does this bother you? Puberty. It's fun to say. Puberty puberty.

It's hard, these routine questions, because in our culture, most of the time, people don't really want to know. So it's important to figure out who's asking and whether they're worth the emotional energy. If they're asking because you have a good relationship and they truly want to know and help, then go with some honesty. Let them know you're hurting and how yeah, heck yeah, they can totally bring you a latte and that sounds great. If they're someone you don't know that well and they're just asking because of some weird Western cultural

Via Facebook @UnexpectedMel

Evie asks questions nonstop all day long. I've started answering with questions, so our conversations have become like a game on *Whose Line Is It Anyway?* First person to answer with a statement is out. #SocraticParentingMethod

Evie: What are we eating for dinner five days from now?

Me: Why do you need to know this?

Evie: We're having pizza, right?

Me: Do you think we're having pizza?

Evie: Are we having dinner?

Me: Do you think that's a good idea?

Evie: Yes.

Me: Ha-HA!

tradition in which we ask meaningless questions and go through the motions of politeness, then no, you don't owe them answers. They aren't awful; they're just performing a dance by rote.

I learned this the hard way, like I learn most things, when we were terrified we'd lost Evie forever. We'd been in the adoption process for almost two years and had received monthly updates and photos of her for almost a year. We'd met her, held her, gazed into her eyes, and gone to court. And our case hit snags as the process seemed to change daily. And we're all for every snag being detangled carefully and ethically for the sake of the child. Absolutely. But the snagging takes a toll.

Via Facebook @UnexpectedMel

Evie: Mommy, I want gum.

Cashier: Aw, she's so cute. How can you say no?

Me: Because I've found the gum smashed in the car, in bed, in hair, in carpet, behind the toilet . . .

Cashier: Oh, you CAN say no.

Me: Uh-huh.

Someone I really like but didn't know very well asked how things were going, and I answered about the snagging. That we might lose her forever.

The friend said, "But you'll still get a child, right?" As if our kids are replaceable and interchangeable.

She didn't think about the enormity of the situation. That Evie might be stuck in an orphanage forever. Permanently in limbo for the rest of her life. And I put this person in a tough situation, hearing a virtual stranger's real pain and feeling the pressure to respond.

I'm learning to choose the right moments for sharing the hard stuff. And sometimes it's just better not to.

It's Okay to Hide

It's okay to stay away from the question askers for a while. I mean, not forever, but for a time, it's okay to hide. And then find your safe people—the ones who ask and wait for an answer—and let them help. Let them be your wingmen, the people who can flank you on all sides. Maintain eye contact with the safe ones and perform March Madness-worthy pick-and-rolls off them to ditch the baddies.

A Note About Safe People

Safe people pick up cues and know when to back off and change the subject.

Safe people can let you lead the conversation and talk about what you need to talk about, not what they need to know.

Safe people give you grace when you're melting down and not handling things perfectly. They understand what's underlying and that it's not them/the cheeseburger you're eating/how your skinny jeans are cutting off circulation.

Safe people check on you when you drop off the face of the earth.

Safe people pray for you but don't use prayers to gossip about you.

Safe people don't use your pain to manipulate you into doing what they want you to do.

Safe people listen well.

Safe people aren't perfect, but they're humble and apologize when they screw up.

Nonverbal Cues

Communication experts like to tell us that as much as 90 percent of our communication with each other is nonverbal. Does that mean I should remove 90 percent of the words in this book and hope you'll get the gist from my author photo? Darn, why didn't I think of that before? Anyhoo, since nonverbal communication is THAT important, I thought I should give you some handy tips for mastering important communication techniques for THOSE people (or to help you interpret them).

Easy steps to mastering Pity Face

1. Tilt ear to the side, drawing your ear to your shoulder slightly. Not so much that it looks like you're stretching.
2. Purse lips.
3. Lift eyebrows.
4. Scrunch eyebrows together.
5. Nod head up and down slightly, like a caring, human bobblehead.
6. Murmur mm-hmms.
7. If your neck gets tired, shift to the other side and continue pitying.

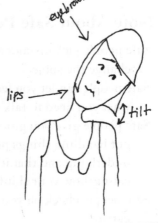

Easy steps to mastering Fake Friendly Face

1. Set smile in medium mode: edges up, no teeth.
2. Let eyes wander to spot on the wall behind the person's left ear.
3. If possible, do not stop walking.
4. Murmur, "So nice to see you," as you pass.

Easy steps to mastering "Don't You Ever Ask Me That Question Again" Face

1. Apply steps 1 and 2 of Fake Friendly Face.
2. Narrow eyes.
3. Slowly slide narrowed eyes to make eye contact with person.
4. Tilt head like Pity Face.

Awkward Hugging

The Doctor: Well you know what they say, "Hugging is a great way to hide your face."

—*Doctor Who*[1]

So there are people with all the words, the good words, the bad words, and how to deal with words, and then there's the physical contact. There are two types of people in the world—the ones who'd rather keep their torsos to themselves and the ones who want to get up on you all the time.

Awkward hugs happen when both types of people find themselves together in an emotionally charged situation, like a funeral or any retreat when the speaker has people stand and receive prayer while the band plays "Oceans."

I'm a hugger. I'll full-frontal boob hug just about anybody, and I like to think of myself as a student of the awkward hug. I hate Pinterest, but I have an entire pin board (Is that what you call it?) dedicated to the curation of awkward hugging moments.

There's Voldemort and Draco at the end of the movie *Harry Potter and the Deathly Hallows, Part II*, when the Dark Lord welcomes Draco onto his team of evildoers while his parents wave him over and all his classmates watch. So awkward. I cringe. In a delicious, voyeuristic way.

There's the Twelfth Doctor and Clara. Every single time. Actually, anytime Twelve hugs anyone ever. He's the antithesis of hugging. (Y'all, if I mention "The Doctor," I'm off on a tangent about *Doctor Who*. I realize not everyone is addicted to this show. I have no explanation for how some people can go whole days without thinking about it, but I acknowledge the fact.)

There's the time I tried to full-frontal hug a male coworker at the church I used to work for. I realized once I got in there that he was a side-hugger and was feeling highly inappropriate, which made me feel inappropriate, and after I disengaged and said good-bye, I wondered if I needed to write his wife a note or something. Poor thing. He seemed traumatized.

When you're going through a difficult time, all kinds of people want to hug you. People like me, who mean well but may foist their boobs on you against your will. You have a few options.

Stand with your arms rigidly at your sides. This will indicate that you are indeed not feeling it, and the hugger will disengage rapidly and make apologies.

Hug them back as hard as you can. Try to perform a little free spinal adjustment. Pick them up if you're really strong. It's a good opportunity to get out some repressed aggression, and they will be trying to get away from you.

Blow your nose into their shirt and breathe "thank you" into their ear. Again, the hug will end. And probably never happen again.

If you see the hug coming on and have time to prepare, pull your arms into your chest before they squeeze, thus basically giving yourself a hug and avoiding maximum full frontal damage.

When they get too close, start describing your ringworm, head lice, or scabies in great detail. Talk about the ointments and creams. Explain about the contagiousness.

Scream, "NO HUGGING!"

You're going through something. You're allowed to be quirky.

The Two Most Powerful Words

Jack: We are lovers.

Liz Lemon: That word bums me out unless it's between the words "meat" and "pizza."

—30 Rock[1]

Okay. Other people can be awful. They can say the wrong thing, ask the wrong question at the wrong time, hug you in the wrong way. But sometimes people are awfully . . . wonderful. And only *other* people can say the two most powerful words.

Sitting in the sunshine watching our kiddos dig in the dirt, my friend shares about struggling with anxiety, that heart-pounding, clenching, can't breathe, suffocating stress. As the words bubble out of her, I nod, murmuring, "Me too." She sighs. "Really? So it's not just me?"

At a restaurant with another adoptive mom, over a steaming plate of chicken tikka masala, I choke out my deepest fear about parenting, the underlying knife hovering by my heart as we struggle with attachment and forging this adoption bond after brokenness. "The thing I fear the most is what if she rejects God as she rejects me?" She whispers, "Me too. I worry about that too."

In his room crumpled on the carpet, my son sobs to me, "Sometimes I just get so mad and I make bad choices, Mommy!" "Me too, sweetheart. Me too." He blinks back tears and looks up at me. I watch as despair drains from his face and something like hope crinkles the side of his mouth.

On the phone with a friend worrying that the daily toil of

marriage is too exhausting, "Sometimes I feel like I want to give up and stop working so hard." "Me, too."

Me too. These may be the two most powerful words in a relationship.

Nothing brings a bigger sigh of relief than knowing that someone understands, that we're not crazy, that we're not beyond hope.

Just a Little Bit Messier than Everyone Else

I often feel just a little bit messier than everyone else, just a little less together, like everyone is a bit shinier than I am, a tad closer to nailing it. When one of these shiny people enters into my overly honest ramblings and offers, "Me too," I realize we're all just people, whether our clothes are ironed and our beds are made, or we live on the wrinkly side of life.

I love these friends, the ones who enter in, who choose to accept my invitation to honest relationship. Here's my hurt, here's my fear, here's my kitchen with the oatmeal bowl from yesterday. Are you ready to show me yours?

Please don't wash my bowl. Don't fix my fear. But please, if you can, share a "Me too."

I want to be a "Me too" friend. I want to be a "Me too" mom and wife. A safe place where people can share their fears and struggles and find refuge and empathy, rather than pity or shame.

Maybe our issues are a little bit different, but we can enter into the sacred space of shared feelings and pain.

We're on the same team. You're not alone. We both struggle, and we can struggle together.

> Are you praying for something and scared that God might not answer the way you want him to? Me too.
> Are you worried you're messing up your kids? Me too.
> Are you still in your jammies as you read this? Me too.

I've been reading through the book of John, and a few days ago I read John 8, when the crowd brings the woman "caught" in adultery to Jesus to stone her and he says something like, "Let he who is without sin throw the first stone." One by one, as they each drop their stones on the ground and walk away, they are really saying, "Me too. I'm a sinner too." Me too. Me too. Me too.

There's commonality in the ways that we fear, and there's commonality in the ways that we fail, and when we partner in the pain, it gives way to sharing in the joy as well.

From the pit of despair to the pinnacle of triumph, I am so glad we have each other on this difficult, dazzling, unexpected ride.

All I Ever Wanted

I never imagined that I would spend two Mother's Days visiting my son behind bars. It was the hardest experience of my life. I feared that my son's life was ruined and mine was following close behind. But if you have walked with the Lord for long, you know that he is the great redeemer. He has enough grace and compassion to cover all our brokenness.

It is so scary for a parent when your children get old enough to make choices for themselves that you have no control over. Choices that can leave scars for them. My son committed a crime. No one was physically hurt, but it was a felony. Early on we thought that because he had never gotten into trouble before that it would be considered a juvenile act. We were wrong. And our story became very public.

It mattered to me what people thought of me. I was the classic good little girl. I obeyed rules, dedicated my life to Christ as a teenager, and strived to be a godly mother. I was crushed for my child. But I was also humiliated beyond words as a parent. I wanted to hide inside my house and never show my face again in public. I retreated from social situations. There were bold friends who initiated the contact, the ones who called us, not waiting for us "to be ready." I expected judgment from others.

Instead I received great compassion. Many came forward with stories of their own that I had never known. I will be forever thankful for those dear ones.

When our children are young, we can pretty much control their environment. We can filter out the bad and protect them. Then they start school and some jerk on the playground wounds them with words. Their world becomes a constant test ground in school and sports. We struggle to convince them of their value and uniqueness. Then they become teenagers, and they are convinced that they know all they need to know and are invincible (especially boys).

There is a constant struggle between young lives moving toward independence and the wisdom of years from a parent's perspective. We know that there are mistakes you can make during the teen years which can dramatically alter the trajectory of a life.

My son was not innocent. And yet my heart broke in pieces as I watched him pay a price that seemed way too severe. We could only see him for four hours on Sunday each week. No calls. No birthday gifts. No visits on Christmas. His sixteenth birthday was spent in a cell instead of standing at the DMV for his driver's license. I have no pictures of him during this time. My biggest fear was that he would emerge from two years in this awful place bitter and schooled as a first-class career criminal.

But God . . . just let those two words sink in. But God, being rich in mercy, the author of redemption, the ultimate repurposer, never abandoned us. There was healing and hope. Now twenty-something years later, it almost seems like a horrible nightmare. A child who only finished ninth grade went on to get a college degree and then a doctorate. He married.

Became a professional. A law-abiding life. He would be your best neighbor.

There are scars, I can't deny that. There will be lifelong trust issues. None of us gets through this life without getting beaten up in some way. But God . . .

—Anonymous

So "me too" is what we should say. As for the rest, as Dr. Evil said, "Zip it. . . . Look! I'm 'Zippy' Longstocking! . . . When a problem comes along, you must zip it! Zip it good!"[2] Or pick something from next chapter's handy-dandy helpful list and go with it. Ready? Me too.

100 Things You Can Do to Help

Salvadore: Encouragement, yes!

—Couples Retreat[1]

If you have a friend going through something hard and you don't know how to help, here are 100 things you could do. And as for you and your own hard stuff, put a check next to the things on this list that work for you and feel free to angrily scratch off the stuff that's complete bunk. What do I know? When it comes to yourself, you know way better than I do.

Obviously, use your judgment, because they all won't apply for your situation. For instance, if your friend is drying out in rehab, do not go with number nine, "Bring over a bottle of wine." You're smart. You'll be able to discern what's best.

1. Give a good, firm, full-frontal hug.
2. Write a note that simply says, "I don't know what to say. This sucks. I love you and I'm praying."
3. Text funny dog memes to them throughout a difficult day.
4. Text prayers to them.
5. Text Bible verses to them, but not the ones that make them feel they have to do something. Just the comforting ones. Unless you really feel something pressing on you. Use your judgment. Don't be lame.
6. Buy a fuzzy blanket and give it as a permanent hug they can wrap around themselves every day.
7. Make a CD or Spotify mix.

8. Make a yummy meal and drop it off.

9. Bring over a bottle of wine.

10. Give a Nerds Rope Bouquet. I hate flowers and have had three people bring me these. So adorable and delicious.

11. Clean their bathroom.

12. Pick them up for church.

13. Bring over their favorite coffee.

14. Take them to a movie.

15. Babysit their kids for an afternoon or evening so they can grab a date night or run errands.

16. Run errands for them.

17. Buy them a massage.

18. If you're broke, give them a back rub yourself. If you don't like touching people, um, maybe use a Hot Wheels car.

19. Research a good counselor in the area. My friend Julie did this for me when I was too messed up to find my own counselor. She found one for me, which took away my excuse not to go.

20. Give the gift of fuzzy socks.

21. Order a pizza to their house.

22. Go over, put your hand on their back or hold a hand, and pray Scripture over them. If this is new and weird for you, you'll find ideas in chapter 24, "A Bunch of Bible Stuff for All Your Various Moods."

23. Buy a book (or books) for them. When I was at the height of Infertility Hell, my friend Stacey shipped me a box filled with books with all different perspectives on the issue. It was awesome. I threw a couple of the books across the room, but a couple of them really helped.

24. Bring a jigsaw puzzle over and work it together.

25. Read funny articles out loud.

26. Binge-watch a show together. Be in charge of snacks, drinks, and pillow fluffing.

27. Don't offer advice. Just listen. There's nothing "just" about that.

28. Let them get angry and don't try to silence them or talk them down right away.
29. Go for a walk together.
30. Paint them a picture.
31. Write verses on index cards and tape them to their bathroom mirrors.
32. Give them a Happiness Basket. My friend Chantel did this for me when I was sad, and it was filled with yellow smiley faces and bendy toys and stickers and stationery and even a little gumball machine.
33. Invite them to an art museum and stand in front of a huge painting together for as long as they want.
34. Put your arm around them.
35. Bring a fresh box of Puffs Plus tissues. The lotion in the Plus is key for combating nasal chaffage.
36. Take their kids somewhere fun, like the zoo or a skating rink or out for pizza. Sometimes the hardest part of going through a rough thing is feeling like your kids are getting the shaft. Knowing they're having fun with people you trust is so freeing.
37. Pull their weeds to freshen up their yard.
38. Bring in the mail and newspapers.
39. Buy fruit and milk, the basics that run out too fast.
40. Candy. Bring their favorite candy.
41. Change the sheets on their beds.
42. Unload the dishwasher.
43. Get a bunch of friends to write encouraging notes.
44. Bring a new makeup bag with face wipes, lip balm, gum, and yummy lotion. My cousin-in-law Coventry did this for me when I was in the hospital, and it's still one of my favorite gifts ever.

Via Twitter @UnexpectedMel

Evie: My bear is hungry.

Me: Okay, let's get bear some food.

Evie: She needs your milk.

Me: I'm not breastfeeding your teddy bear.

45. Give them a pedicure—soak their feet, massage their calves, and paint their toenails.
46. Sit in silence next to them. Just be there without expectations.
47. Open their curtains and let the sunshine in.
48. Bring over a new puppy for them to snuggle temporarily.
49. Invite them to an outdoor concert. Pack a picnic.
50. Wash their car.
51. Write notes of encouragement and hide them in drawers and pockets where they'll find them.
52. Write a stack of letters that are sealed and dated, one per day or week, to get them through a hard time. I did this for Ana when she had to return to Latvia after visiting us all summer. I drew funny pictures and looked up Russian words and made her enough sealed envelopes to open one a week till Christmas.
53. Text them silly animated gifs.
54. Go with them to their appointment and hold their purse, pants, book, whatever. Be their holder.
55. Pick up their kids from school and swing through the drive-thru for ice cream on the way home.
56. Order their favorite Bible verse or saying as a wall sticker.
57. Empty all their trash cans and take the trash out.
58. Leave an encouraging message on their phone that they can listen to over and over.
59. Come over and brush their hair. (Um, this one's for me. Please somebody, come brush my hair. I'm willing to pay money for this service.)
60. Go for a drive. If you live in the city, drive out together. If you live out, drive into the city. Roll down the windows and let them feel the wind on their face.
61. Blast eighties music and have a dance party in the kitchen together.
62. Bring something potatoey. Potatoes are God's greatest comfort food. Fried, chipped, mashed, boiled. I mean, I could go all Bubba Gump Shrimp Co. on y'all about this.

63. Wash and fold a load of towels. People are weird about their clothes. We all know which ones go in the dryer and which ones hang dry. But towels are fairly universal. It's usually safe to do a load of towels for someone.

64. Offer to coordinate meals. If something's going on that's going to be a long road, like your friend or her child is undergoing cancer treatments, set up an online meal sign-up and invite everyone to take a day or two. Most people don't need meals delivered every night, but every other night or even a couple times a week can really help when they're spending long hours at the hospital.

65. Drop off a bag of groceries on the doorstep.

66. Slip a gift card into their bag when they aren't looking.

67. Stand near them in public when you know they're freaking out about being around people and be prepared to catch a signal to run interference for them.

68. Keep their secrets and be trustworthy.

69. Deliver a bag filled with paper plates, cups, and plastic cutlery with a note that says, "Throw these away guilt-free. You can save the environment later. I'm giving you the gift of no dirty dishes. I'm the bad waster, not you. It's on me. Use the crap out of these things and chuck 'em out with a clean conscience."

70. Ask open-ended questions that let them externally process everything.

71. Let them guide the conversation.

72. If they seem to be needing advice, clarify by saying, "Are you asking for my advice?" If the answer is yes, start with, "Okay, if it were me, I would _____," and end with, "But that's just me. What are you thinking?"

73. Give them a journal and write verses and encouraging words on random pages throughout it.

74. If they need to take a break from people but can't find the strength to set a boundary, offer to be responsible for their phone for a night.

75. Snail mail a non-cheesy greeting card. If you can only find cheesy ones, make liberal use of a Sharpie and alter it for your purposes.

76. Lots of people bring dinner, so try breakfast in a box. Bagels, cream cheeses, mini cereal boxes for the kids, breakfast bars, yogurts. Or if they have school-aged kids, bring items they can use to pack their own lunches, like string cheese and premade sandwiches and crackers.

77. Invite them to church and sit by them so they don't feel weird. Never, ever elbow them or call attention to them, even if the pastor practically shouts the exact verse for their exact situation.

78. Help their kids with homework. Sign their folders and help them pack their backpacks for the next day.

79. If they have a CaringBridge site or blog keeping people up on what's going on, leave a comment. I promise you they're reading every single one.

80. Have your kids draw a picture and stick it in their mailbox.

81. Warm up a heating pad and bring it to them on the couch.

82. Proofread their resume and help them pull everything together to nail upcoming interviews.

83. Pray for the right words and timing if you need to talk about something hard, like a problem you see or interventiony stuff. Search yourself and double-check your heart and your own motives before you move in that direction.

84. If you have to say something hard because you love them so much and see danger signs whizzing all over the place, think about if it was you and confront as ye wish to be-ith confronted.

85. Check in and don't disappear on them.

86. Be honest if you have your own stuff going on. You're not a freaking saint.

87. Take Buzzfeed quizzes together and snort-laugh.

88. Fiercely debate which song you'd pick for a lip-sync battle with Jimmy Fallon.

89. Take them with you to serve at the local food bank. Get their mind off their own stuff for a couple hours and focus on helping others.

90. If you aren't a hugger and you aren't super duper close to this person, give an elbow squeeze. An elbow is always a safe bet and keeps your boobies to yourself while allowing a moment of physical reassurance.

91. Say, "I'm sorry. I got nothin'. I'm so sorry." Then hug them. Repeat as needed. No need to solve anything.

92. Buy them a fresh pack of Sharpies, a pad of paper, some sticky notes, and a roll of tape. Everyone loves new office supplies.

93. Print photos of good times and paste them in a little scrapbook. During hard stuff, it's hard to (a) remember the good things and (b) find the energy and time to scrapbook.

94. Surprise them with a cupcake one afternoon.

95. Text them first thing in the morning (when you know they're already up) to let them know you're thinking about them.

96. Write a "Top 10 Things I Love About You" list for them. Or for a birthday, use their age, "33 Things I Like About You."

97. Offer to grab toiletries next time you're out. A lot of people don't want to bother you, but if you say, "Hey, I'm headed to Target. Need anything while I'm there?" they're more willing to give you a couple of things for your list.

98. De-turd their yard if they have dogs. It's the ultimate expression of love.

99. Invite their kids to have a sleepover at your house to give them a whole overnight free.

100. Light a candle for them all afternoon and say a prayer every time you see the candle. Tell them you're doing this. My friend Fabiola taught me this. She'd text me, "I lit a candle for you and am praying." It meant the world.

-PART-
FIVE

On God, Suffering, and Other Easy Subjects

The Part of the Book Where We Try to Make Sense of Something That's Way Beyond Our Pay Grade

Her Cupcake Is Better Than Mine

Remember how I mentioned that "It's not fair!" is the heart-cry of the entire human race? Well, the it's-not-fair-ocity rages so strongly in our house that Alex and I finally put the kibosh on saying it. That hasn't thwarted our inventive children, who now mutter "I.N.F." under their breaths. We can stop them from saying it . . . technically, anyway . . . but we can't stop them from feeling it.

My children are three different ages, two different genders, and come from three different continents. Their early childhoods, personalities, and needs are as diverse as the big, big world in which we live. We would do a disservice to them to parent them the same because they aren't the same. Each one is unique, as is our approach to parenting.

My kids hate this. In theory, they want everything exactly the same. But do they really know what they're asking for? It's not fair. Okay, well, then, shall I have the ten-year-old have a quiet time in the afternoon like the five-year-old? (This is actually an amazing idea. Why don't I do this!?) Should the eight-year-old be expected to learn division like the ten-year-old?

Fair is an impossible standard. I wonder if God feels the same way. I know, I know, there is no such thing as impossible when it

161

comes to God. He made everything. Nothing is too big. But as our omnipotent parent, God could make us all the same and make our circumstances the same, but he doesn't. He parents each one of us individually.

The summer after my freshman year of college, I was getting on a plane for my first overseas mission trip, and my mom gave me *Disappointment with God* by Philip Yancey. I devoured it. He asks three questions: "Is God unfair? Is God silent? Is God hidden?" Honestly, as I reread it in preparation for this book, I wondered why I bothered writing about unfairness at all, when Yancey had written such a wonderful resource. (But this book quotes *Tommy Boy*, so, you know, important.) My faith has never been the same since I read, "God learns how to be a parent." Yancey qualifies that mind-blowing statement with a footnote:

> A phrase like "God learns" may seem strange because we normally think of learning as a mental process, moving in sequence from a state of not-knowing to a state of knowing. God, of course, is not bound by time or ignorance. He "learns" in the sense of taking on new experiences, such as the creation of free human beings. Using the word in a similar sense, Hebrews says that Jesus "learned obedience from what he suffered."[2]

Yancey made me think about God's relationship with his people in Genesis as this evolving, parent-child relationship. He doled out individualized punishments and felt the emotions we feel as human parents: "God has deep emotions; he feels delight and frustration and anger."[3]

Over the last couple decades since reading this book for the first time, I've mulled over this parent-child relationship and how, even today, long after Adam and Eve and Noah and Abraham, God really does parent us individually. Our covenant with Jesus is the same, we're all saved by the same death and resurrection, but the things that happen to us in life and our combination of circumstances are incredibly different.

And it's not fair. It's never fair. Nothing is fair. If you have more than one kid, like God, you've probably encountered this challenge.

Ticked-Off Children

Last week I took out each of my kids for an after-school treat. Three kids, three different dates, on three different days. You see where this is going, don't you? You can already tell what happened and are calling me an idiot up in your head.

I receive that. Yep. The dates themselves were fabulous. For whole minutes one-on-one, each child enjoyed some personal love in the form of sugar and my undivided attention. They were happy and felt special.

And then, one-by-one, we'd return home and each child would compare his or her minutes and sugar to the minutes and sugar of siblings. After three days of intentional kid-dating, I found myself with three ticked-off children crying about cupcakes and ice cream.

Via Facebook @UnexpectedMel

This just in: child's summer is COMPLETELY RUINED when Georgia parent asks child to complete one chore before going out to play. The week at the beach means nothing. This is the final straw. Nothing good will ever happen again and child's entire existence is horrible. When questioned about the heinous chore, mom said, "After months and months of endless fun, the craft cabinet needed to be straightened." Child unable to comment as child sobbed uncontrollably and lamented every piece of construction paper and plastic bead.

"Why did *sheeee* get ice cream?"

"Why didn't *I* get a cookie?"

"You never let *meee* get that."

All together now, "It's. Not. Fair."

What I'm discovering about parenting, and through parenting, about myself is that so often we don't have a problem with what we have. We have a problem with comparison.

Why I'm Completely Hacked God Didn't Make Me a Singer

Sometimes I can't believe God didn't make me a singer. A real-life, leopard-print-pants-wearing, electric-guitar-strumming singer who belts out amped-up rock songs and flips her big sweaty hair around the stage. I would rock so hard on *The Tonight Show* and get to meet Jimmy Fallon and then get home in time to lead worship at church because, of course, *of course*, I'd do it all for the glory of the Lord. Duh. Of course.

Or an incredible actor. I could be Emma Stone and have epic lip-sync battles and still enjoy the aforementioned meeting of The Fallon. The sexy raspy voice would be gravy on top of the Thanksgiving feast of my awesomesauce life.

Instead, my voice is decidedly un-raspy and un-melodic. I could try chain-smoking, but instead of Emma Stone, I think I'd end up sounding more like Estelle, Joey Tribbiani's agent on *Friends*.

Via Twitter @UnexpectedMel

Evie: I asked God to make me a princess. Why isn't he doin' that thing?

For most of my life, I felt extremely discontented with the gifts God gave me. I adore writing and I like speaking and feel tremendously motivated and passionate about orphan care and justice issues. I love gleaning wisdom from the Bible and connecting people with each other.

But I can't rock out on stage with my awesome singing voice and rad guitar, so I'm lame. I also can't seem to put photos in albums, make plants grow in the ground, or execute sports of any kind. What a loser.

I always thought there was something wrong with me or that I was made lesser, not as awesome as other people. It took me about thirty-five years to discover the elementary truth that God makes us all different.

We know this, but when another girl is rocking out onstage to "Love Is a Battlefield," sometimes we just want to be her and think God loves us just a little bit less because we aren't.

Killing Ourselves with Comparison

God loving us just a little bit less. Hmm, that strikes a nerve for me. How about you? Early on in my Christian life, I thought God loved me less because I was a girl.

I grew up wishing I was a boy. It seemed like boys had all the fun. Boys got to be funnier. They'd stand up in front of class for a presentation and goof off and everyone died laughing, including the teachers. There were more roles for them in the school musicals, they had their photos on the front page of the local paper for football every week, and they got to be in charge of everything.

I started reading the Bible and discovered these verses about women being silent and submissive, and rather than asking people what it all meant, I just figured boys were better and got really petulant with God about it. He made me the wrong gender. (Parents and youth group leaders: for the love of God, explain these verses to young women. Spend some serious time here.)

As newlyweds, we took a test to determine our "spiritual gifts," like a Meyers-Briggs test or those old quizzes from *BOP Magazine*. It was like a Buzzfeed quiz for church people. Instead of "Which *Game of Thrones* character are you?" it was "How has God gifted you to serve the church?" I got "pastor/shepherd." And then people told me that since I was a girl, that meant working with kids or leading a women's group. I figured they'd also probably let me lead some sheep if I wanted to. Or at least the ewes.

Anyway, at first I thought God loved me less because I was a girl, then later on I thought he loved me less because I was a girl who couldn't fulfill her calling to get pregnant and have bouncing Christian babies.

By the time I made it through high school and a few boyfriends, I felt overwhelmed by my inability to perform perfectly, to follow the rules exactly, to color inside the lines. My hips were too big, my zits too numerous, and I had too many opinions to be a demure, likable girl. I was weird, and I wasn't comfortable enough in my own skin yet to think weird was awesome.

So of course the only logical thing to do was stop eating and develop a raging eating disorder. One day, I realized that I couldn't remember the last time I had eaten, and in that moment of realization, I decided that I didn't deserve food anymore. I liked hurting myself a little too much.

Food was for lovable people. I wasn't worth food. All the better people could eat. I'd just be over here trying to earn love.

I tried so hard to nail perfection on its impossibly tiny head, but the older I got, the more I was confronted by my not-enough-ed-ness.

Amy's Story: I'm Pretty Sure I Had a Midlife Crisis

I always thought I'd be more established by now. That we wouldn't still have debt, that we wouldn't still fight about the same things we did when we were younger, that I'd be more influential or more well-known or more knowledgeable than I am, or that I'd be an expert on something by now. We've been married for twenty years, and I turned forty-one this year.

I'm pretty sure I had a midlife crisis a year ago. Sure, we don't have bad debt, we don't fight as much, and we do understand each other better after all these years, and I'm probably more influential than I realize . . . especially to my four kiddos. I guess the point is that when you're younger, you have ideas of how you think your life will be when you're forty, and I think most people could say without a doubt it won't look like how you pictured it. But if you make it to forty, you should be thankful for whatever you have or have accomplished because God saw fit for you to be around for forty years.

—Amy O.

When I was growing up, my mother warned me that if I was anything like she was, all I'd have to do is hang my clothes near a boy in order to get pregnant. She was just that fertile, so warning warning warning don't have sex or you'll get pregnant. It was a mostly effective deterrent, but eventually, after the long walk down a rose-petaled aisle, it was time.

Even though I was on the pill, I was terrified that I'd get pregnant on my honeymoon. I mean, if I was just that fertile, then it could happen at any moment. A single sperm could probably fly through the air, do *The Amazing Race* up my hoo-ha, and make a baby without my knowledge.

A couple years into marriage, I decided that might not be so bad, so I reckoned it was time to knock me up. The first time I had sex after going off the pill, I knew. Pregnant. I was soooo fertile. I was the Tigris and Euphrates. I was the Fertile Crescent of fertility.

But I didn't get my mother's fertility. Month after month, year after year, I watched other women's bellies blow up with babies and mine stayed flat. I wouldn't have the experience of the pee stick turning blue. I wouldn't give my husband the good news. All the dreams of how it would be came crashing down in a smoldering heap at my feet. I told God, "It's not fair."

Why did women who didn't want to get pregnant have babies while people like me couldn't? I didn't understand.

I compared myself to women sporting healthy baby bellies and wondered if they worked out more, ate better, or prayed harder. Maybe I was too dried up from those previous years of anorexia. I wasn't enough. I was less than. They were better.

Ugh, have you ever caught yourself feeling that way? We kill ourselves with comparison.

Fertility Showdown 2000 . . . BC

I think one of the strangest accounts in the Bible—strange to my twenty-first-century eyes—is the birth of the twelve tribes of Israel and the fertility competition between Jacob's wives, Leah and Rachel. Rachel had all his love and Leah had all the fertility, and that right there is a recipe for disaster. At least as I was wandering through my own infertility, I wasn't freaking out that Alex loved his other wife more. So my heart goes out to Leah, unloved and unwanted. And I'm touched that God saw her situation and gave her babies. "When the LORD saw that Leah was not loved, he enabled her to conceive" (Genesis 29:31). But then my heart shifts to Rachel and breaks because, though she's loved by her husband, "Rachel remained childless" (v. 31 again).

So unloved Leah birthed Reuben, Simeon, Levi, and Judah. And "when Rachel saw that she was not bearing Jacob any children, she became jealous of her sister" (Genesis 30:1). Wouldn't you? This stunk like the inside of a *Star Wars* Tauntaun. "'So she said to Jacob, 'Give me children, or I'll die!'" (v. 1 again).

And then Jacob got mad at her and said, "Am I in the place of God, who has kept you from having children?" (Genesis 30:2). Okay, lemme stop you right there, Jacob. First, have some freaking compassion on your wife, whom you love. I mean, your loving her, *only her*, has created a lot of this angst. And second, you're saying God caused her infertility? Mkay, ima file that away to chew on for the rest of forever, and I'll have some questions for God when I get to heaven.

So Rachel ups the ante and gives him Bilhah, her servant, to serve as a surrogate. But they didn't have reproductive endocrinologists back then, so surrogacy worked the old-fashioned way, with actual sex instead of sterilized turkey basters. So Team Rachel and Bilhah had Dan and Naphtali, who, by the way, was named for "I have had a struggle with my sister, and I have won" (Genesis 30:8). And Leah saw what was going on and got her servant, Zilpah, in on this. Team Leah and Zilpah had Gad and Asher.

And then Rachel wanted some of Leah's son's mandrakes and bartered her night for sex with Jacob for some mandrakes. (Note: Mandrakes were thought to aid conception, so Rachel was trying to get her hands on fertility herbs. One time when the pharmacy was out of the injections I needed and I thought we'd have to flub a whole round of intrauterine insemination, I felt about this desperate. I would've done just about anything for mandrakes.) This next part is straight out of Melanie's *NIV: StagePlay* version:

> Rachel: Please give me some of your son's mandrakes.
> Leah: Wasn't it enough that you took away my husband?
>   Will you take my son's mandrakes too?
> Rachel: Very well, he can sleep with you tonight in return
>   for your son's mandrakes.
> Leah (*to Jacob*): You must sleep with me. I have hired you
>   with my son's mandrakes.
> Jacob: (*blink blink*)

(Genesis 30:14–16. Really. Look it up.)

(There's not a lot to say. Um. Pimping Jacob out for some kind of leafy herb with an anthropomorphic root said to have magical powers. He didn't seem to mind. This is biblical marriage.)

Then Genesis says, "God listened to Leah" (30:17). Which tells me to keep praying. Oddly, it does not tell me to hire my husband for sex using vegetables, which to be fair, is my issue. So Leah has Issachar, then Zebulun. (Then Dinah, a daughter, for the win!) (Poor Dinah. It does not end well for her.)

"Then God remembered Rachel; he listened to her and enabled her to conceive" (v. 22). I'm not sure if he'd forgotten or it

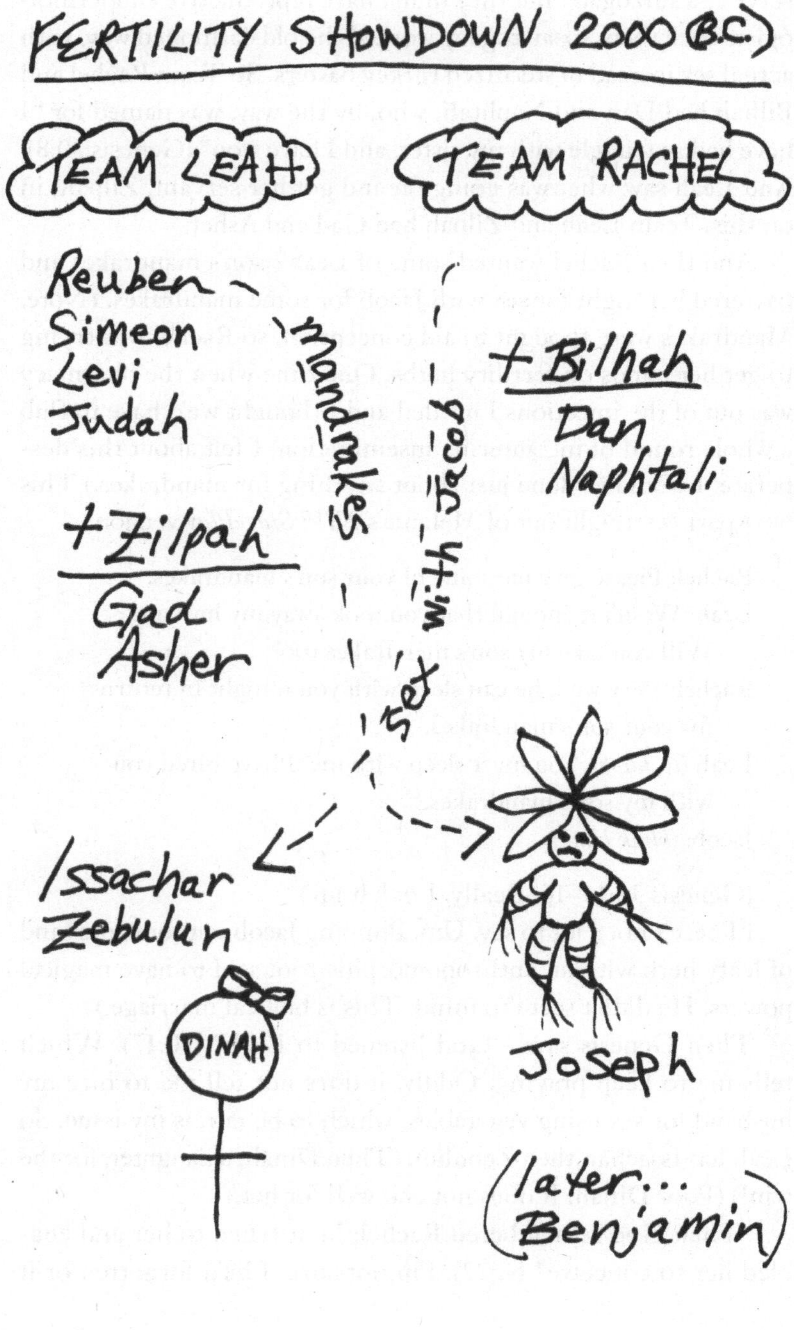

FERTILITY SHOWDOWN 2000 (B.C.)

TEAM LEAH

Reuben
Simeon
Levi
Judah

+ Zilpah
Gad
Asher

Issachar
Zebulun

DINAH

TEAM RACHEL

+ Bilhah
Dan
Naphtali

Mandrakes

Sex with Jacob

Joseph

(later...
Benjamin)

was just finally time. I'd like to believe the latter. She named her son Joseph.

Throughout Fertility Showdown 2000 . . . BC, Leah was motivated by this: "This time my husband will treat me with honor" (Genesis 30:20). And Rachel was motivated by this: "God has taken away my disgrace" (v. 23). Love and babies. These women were killing themselves with comparison. And God heard and listened . . . and let it all happen—the lack of love, the barrenness, the competition. It's still happening today.

Her cupcakes are cuter, her hair is fluffier, and she always balances her checkbook. Her kids are better behaved, she's on the fast track to management, and she wears wedge heels like a boss. Comparison will drive you beyond bonkers.

Let's give up. When I stop looking across the street and start looking at my own dang Facebook page, my eyes adjust to the reality of my own set of pixels. And they're really quite nice.

I'm not less than, and neither are you. There's no *better*. We're all *best*.

Now, years later, after in vitro and adoptions (no mandrakes required), I have children bouncing down the halls of my house, and I've made a discovery that's so personal, so difficult to explain, and so not what I wanted to hear back then.

God makes beauty from ashes.

But first everything has to burn down.

You Went to the Zoo

Will Stronghold: If life were suddenly to get fair, I doubt it would happen in high school.

—*Sky High*[1]

The summer I was thirteen, my family road-tripped our silver Taurus station wagon with burgundy interior all over the Wild, Wild West. We drove from our suburb of Cleveland over to St. Louis, to Denver, and then all around Utah, New Mexico and Arizona, then back across through Wyoming and South Dakota.

That was the golden age of teen summer movies, and I'd seen *The Great Outdoors, Meatballs, Meatballs Part II, Space Camp, Summer School,* et alia, and I knew exactly what was going to happen on this trip. I was going to find the cutest boy in America and kiss him at one of those lookout points along the highway overlooking the Painted Desert or something. I would make my teen summer romance memories, and I would have something seriously exciting to journal about in my writing spot in the closet where I went to brood and pen moody poetry.

There was one tiny wrinkle in my plan. My parents were enthralled with the national parks, and the places we visited on our western trip were consistently packed with the over-sixty-five crowd. I spent two weeks surrounded by silver-haired retirees, and my chances of summer lovin' grew slimmer by the day.

It didn't help that what we thought was just altitude sickness at the summit of Pike's Peak turned out to be strep throat, and the only action I got consisted of my mom shoving suppositories up my butt in dingy motel rooms until my fever finally broke.

Let's pretend that last paragraph didn't happen. That's gross, even for me.

We stayed at the Stanley Hotel in Estes Park, apparently a mecca for senior citizens on the loose. And the inspiration for *The Shining*. REDRUM. (Now I know why Jack Nicholson went mad. That place is crazy dull.) At Mount Rushmore, we got to go to a concert, and I was pretty excited, until I realized it was what we dubbed The Choir from Hell. My summer concert experience was a robed chorus.

You can almost feel the eyeball rolls jumping off the page, can't you? I was too cool for school in the backseat of the Taurus, poo-pooing the Grand Canyon ("Yep. There it is."), and refusing to get out of the car to hike up another trail because Teen-Too-Tired and Everything Was Lame.

Via Twitter @UnexpectedMel

Elliott: Wait, middle school is the one after high school, right?

Me: No, middle school is in the middle. Elementary, middle, then high school.

Elliott: So when's old school? I don't want to go there.

We did go white-water rafting in Moab, Utah, where I projected all my thwarted feelings of teen romantic angst on our tanned Teva-sporting guide. He was unimpressed, which was surprising, because what bronzed college-aged river rafter wouldn't be interested in a junior high girl with glasses and braces? Glasses AND braces AND acne. I was a triple threat, sporting the teen triumvirate of radness.

Back home, I listened to friends talk about vacays to the beach, and I brooded over the unfairness of my vacation with the senescent. The following summer my parents finally took us to the beach, where I found not one, but two, cute boys to kiss and got my summer romance after all.

Oh, and when you're done with this book, please burn it. We'll need to burn all the books before my daughters read this part and think I'm saying this kind of behavior is acceptable. Girls, make better choices. National parks are the bomb diggity. Hang out with the elderly.

Somewhere in the Badlands I put my foot through the front windshield of the Taurus. Here's my brother pointing out the damage while I sob hysterically. My mom is rocking Calgon Take Me Away Face like a boss.

Woo and hoo, Sedona, Arizona. I wore my very best
tie-dyed flour sack held up with scrunchies on your
behalf. Yawn, all this picture posing is exhausting.

Brittany's Story: He Isn't Finished Writing Yet

Throughout my life there have been many journeys God has
asked me to go on. Some easier and some much more difficult.
Growing up, I went through a lot of periods of my life that
didn't feel fair. When you're younger, those things happen—
when your crayon breaks or you scrape your knee—but these
aren't the trials I'm talking about.

My freshman year of high school, my world as I knew it fell
apart. My parents split up, and my dad moved a couple miles
away. It was heartbreaking to watch this go on in my own
home. It was one of those situations I thought would never

happen to me. It was that time when I thought that would be my hardest journey.

Two years later, God put me on a completely different path. Things had been going downhill with my dad. He was an alcoholic, and the choices he was making were leading him down a dark path. One of which I always thought he'd come back from. "He'll bounce back like he always does," I thought. "Things will get better, he'll be okay," I told myself over and over again, trying to justify the situation.

May 6, 2013, was the day my life changed forever. I learned my dad had passed away, and my heart broke into a million pieces. My world was broken. I thought I would have more time. What I would give to have one last conversation or even to see him one last time. But I had to remind myself God had a plan for my mom, my brother, and me. Somehow I had to trust him that we were going to be okay.

I'm not going to say the time since then has been easy, because it sure hasn't been. I've struggled a lot in my faith, I've questioned God, and I've wondered if this is all worth it. I know in my heart God is working through me every day and will continue to use me. He's still writing my story, pen in hand. When I fall, he picks me up and the journey continues. At my breaking points, he's shown me that he's still here, and he isn't leaving. There are a lot of times where we fall on our knees and question God. We tell him life isn't fair. This isn't how things are supposed to go! But God is the author of this story, he's writing our journey, and if we can't see a clear ending in sight, it just might be that he isn't finished writing yet.

—*Brittany B.*

You Went to the Zoo

The thing is, I spent my whole life thinking about the stuff that happened to me and my own personal unfairness. My mom and I had a stock phrase when I was growing up, kind of a running inside joke. We'd say, "Well, you went to the zoo," meaning, "It isn't fair." Because every single year of elementary school, the class above me would go on a cool field trip. The next year, I'd get psyched up to do that same cool field trip, but the plans would fall through, and my class would end up at the Cleveland Zoo. Every year this happened. It was still a field trip. I was still a middle-class good student with friends, two parents who loved each other, and a decent dirt bike. But I went to the zoo every year, so my life wasn't fair.

And growing up didn't exactly cure me of this mopey zoo-thinking, especially when I encountered the hard stuff. The zoo seemed like a big deal when I was ten, and so my adult big deals are exactly that. They're big. All our stuff is big to us and deserves attention and caring and delicacy.

But over the last few years, I've started looking up from my own darn zoo pass and noticing the lives around me. You probably started that long ago. You're probably way better than I am. What can I say, I'm a really slow learner. But eventually, I realized lots of people were experiencing colossal pain on a level I could barely wrap my brain around.

And colossal pain can stir up some colossally big questions.

Why Do Bad Things Happen?

> Clara: (*angry*) You walk our Earth, Doctor, you breathe our air.
> You make us your friend, and that is your moon, too. And you
> can d*mn well help us when we need it.
>
> Doctor: I was helping.
>
> Clara: What, by clearing off?
>
> Doctor: Yes.
>
> —*Doctor Who*[1]

Lately I have felt like God has left the building. One day in the van when I was driving by myself, I told him out loud with my throat burning hot, "You gave me these kids after all this work and now you've abandoned me, like 'Good luck with that.' Is this a joke to you? I begged and begged for children and you finally relented and now I'm on my own? I got what I asked for?"

My head doesn't agree with this. My head has Bible verses that convince me otherwise. But my heart feels this way sometimes. I know not to trust my feelings. Feelings can lie. But I feel alone and the feeling sucks.

I see what my kids have gone through and what they go through and I'm helpless to heal our home and then I look around and get overwhelmed by the suffering in the world. So much pain.

What Am I Going to Do About It?

Why does God allow bad things to happen? I don't know. I've tried everything. Being mad at him. Being super-obedient and butt-kissing with him, like this is what I wanted and it feels good to suffer. I've even tried not believing in him. For like a second. I can't not believe in him. I can doubt, but I can't not believe because where would I go? The number of things I'd have to unbelieve is so overwhelming that it makes more sense to stick with him and trust that he's real and present in my life. I love how Nadia Bolz-Weber described her faith in *Pastrix*: "I cannot pretend, as much as sometimes I would like to, that I have not throughout my life experienced the redeeming, destabilizing love of a surprising God."[2]

So I've tried not believing in God and failed miserably. I make a terrible atheist. But maybe you've had more success than I have. Maybe you used to believe, experienced suffering, and now you don't, because why would a good God allow such terribleness in the world? If that's you, I'm nodding my head at you and listening. I get it, at least I think I do.

Even though I can get really frustrated at God, I can't write him off completely, because even though I don't know the why, I do know the where. I don't know why he allows the bad stuff, but I know where he positions himself in it. God enters into our suffering. He sent Jesus, who suffered on a cross. When I'm suffering, I can't seem to move away from him. It's the opposite. I feel closer to my suffering Savior, who suffered for me and knows what I'm going through. I don't know why, but I know where. Right beside me.

It might not feel like it, but God cares about your suffering. I'm really, really sure about this because he re-convinces me of this regularly. I don't know why he's letting it happen or what his exact role in the whole thing is or if he's ever going to give you relief, but I know that he cares. Because of Jesus. I love this quote from Philip Yancey in *Where Is God When It Hurts?*:

The fact that Jesus came to earth where he suffered and died does not remove pain from our lives. But it does show that God did not sit idly by and watch us suffer in isolation. He became one of us. Thus, in Jesus, God gives us an up-close and personal look at his response to human suffering. All our questions about God and suffering should, in fact, be filtered through what we know about Jesus.[3]

This is why when I'm hurting I go to the Gospels. I read about Jesus. Because even though I don't know what God will *do* about my pain, I do know how he *feels* about it.

I once heard this from someone who lost his son: "The secret things belong to the LORD our God, but the things revealed belong to us and to our children forever, that we may follow all the words of this law" (Deuteronomy 29:29). The *why* is a secret thing, a hidden thing. That's hard when we want answers. But I'm oddly comforted that God acknowledges some things are secret.

I don't know why God allows awful things to happen. To me, to the people I love, or to the hurting people around the globe. Something about us living in a broken world. I guess the question I always ask myself is, what am I going to do about it? Bad things happen. Because . . . I don't know. But they happen whether I understand them or not, and understanding the *why* is way over my pay grade, so what am I going to do about it? What's my part of the solution?

A lot of my part of the solution is what I talked about in the last part of the book, the things we can do to help. It's being a good friend to the people in my life. But over the last few years, I've started thinking about the other people, the ones not in my daily life, but the ones with whom I share a planet. As I lifted my eyes from my own issues, I discovered a whole other realm where people work in slavery, where children are too hungry to go to school, where whole villages are forced into dependence, and where people are dying of preventable diseases.

From My Own Unfairness to Everybody Else's

When I started asking myself this question, "What's my part of the solution?" I thought maybe I was supposed to rescue people. Like I was the cavalry for people living in slavery and extreme poverty. I just needed to pull my white savior complex up onto my white horse and ride around the world. Oops. Yuck.

What I've come to learn is that I'm not a very good horse rider, and people don't need me on a horse. People don't need me to rescue them. They need me to care enough to partner with them so they can rescue themselves.

When I flip the question from "Why does God allow bad things to happen?" to "What's my part in finding the solution?" I feel empowered to help. I roll up my sleeves, get in the ditch, and do the work of making this world a little better, one choice at a time.

After I discovered that people were living in slavery and poverty, I went through a series of emotions. First, horror. How could this be? How could this kind of evil and brokenness exist in the world? Second, guilt. How the hello did I not know about it, and have I been living with a fuzzy little blindfold on my whole life? Have these verses about helping the poor and widows and orphans been in the Bible the whole time? Are you sure? Third, shame. I stunk. I was an awful, guilty, horrible person complaining about over-roasted coffee beans and how the ice maker on my fridge kept breaking for no good reason.

Horror, guilt, shame. Those emotions broke my heart in all the best ways, but serving others out of horror, guilt, and shame is a terrible idea. It's the birth of a new way of living, but not the way you live. So after that cycle, where do you go?

Determination, discovery, partnership, and relationship. Get over yourself and learn stuff. And then it gets awesome.

When we began the adoption process with Evie and discovered millions of kids living without families, I realized we couldn't adopt them all, and even if we could, that wasn't a good solution. How could I help kids thrive right where they are? Through a friend, I heard about HopeChest, a community transformation and child-development program. HopeChest partners a community in North America with a community in the developing world to form a relationship that will transform them both. It empowers local leaders to address the holistic needs of orphaned and vulnerable children and focuses on sustainability and independence.

Local leaders look at the assets of each unique community and create development plans, which go through three stages: Survive, Thrive, and Succeed. In Survive, they focus on things like child sponsorship, clean water, meeting spiritual and emotional needs, nutrition, and basic medical care. They begin by establishing a "CarePoint," a central location where the children can gather, eat, and meet with local disciplers. Thrive helps with educational support and emergency and preventative medical solutions. Succeed is a launch pad, focusing on income-generating activities, agriculture projects, leadership skills, and vocational training. And we as the partnering communities get to engage in relationships. We work humbly, going in asking, "How can we help?" rather than "Here's what we'll do." This is about sustainability, not creating dependence, and the goal is that someday soon they won't need our help at all. We are not the leaders, or the teachers, or the workers. We are the relationshippers, the cheerleaders, the faithful friends. We get the glorious role of being the sidekicks as the superheroes tackle poverty and injustice in their own towns.

I started learning what people in a village in northern Uganda needed to help break the cycle of poverty and discovered that the greatest hope for orphaned and vulnerable children is creating a safe, healthy community around them. Then I hopped a plane.

I don't know why God lets bad things happen, but I've learned a lot from the widows and orphaned children in Uganda about how to respond to the bad things.

(First, I want to mention here that in Uganda, I've stayed in the nicest resort I've ever seen. The food was spectacular and there was a gorgeous magazine-worthy wedding going on, and Lake Victoria was shimmering as a backdrop. My room was like something out of a movie, and even the mosquito nets were fancy. There were flowers everywhere and horseback riding and really fancy people from all over the world. So when I think of Uganda, I don't just think poverty or violence or whatever the news has to say about it.

And the people I work with in Uganda have more education than I do, more business savvy, more training. They are leaders and college graduates and directors and nurses and teachers and pastors. And they're doing all the work. I shouldn't have to say any of that, but I think between the news and we bloggers writing only about poverty, sometimes we give the wrong impression. To sum up: The developing world does not need us to "save" it. Africa is not a country. Uganda is more than what you see on the news. If anyone would like to take me on a blogger trip to showcase the gorgeous resorts, I am all in.)

In this village in northern Uganda where I've seen God do amazing things, I've developed relationships with the elders, widows, and orphaned children who are working so hard to bring hope and sustainable income to the area. They have struggled with extreme poverty because of violence and disease, and through that struggle they've taught me how to respond when bad things happen. They are my teachers, and here's what I've learned from them.

Find humor in suffering. The second time I visited the kids, they performed a play for us. The actors reenacted the battle with a neighboring tribe that had wiped out so many of their parents. They'd fashioned guns out of scraps of metal and the entire audience shrieked with laughter as they faked death in the dirt. My eyes widened and I tried to smile because they were beaming and excited to share this piece of history with us, and inside I was freaking out over the horror of what these kids had been through.

But it taught me something. They lived it, so they got to laugh about it. On their own terms. They'd taken the thing that had decimated them, destroyed their parents, and left them with nothing, and they'd used it for their own entertainment and remembrance.

I do the same thing. As I've already said, my husband and I tell infertility jokes around our house that would horrify an outsider, but these jokes are how we've coped. When I make fun of my body being a "reproductive nightmare," I'm in control of my own narrative, and I'm refusing to let it get me down. I've heard people talk about "cancer humor" and the macabre laughter in hospital rooms. When my dad almost died, we were quipping the next day. Because laughter about life's trauma is one way to get through, and sometimes when your crying muscles need a rest, your smile muscles are there to take over and give you a break.

My friends in Uganda taught me about faith too. Their faith inspires me. I see them asking for healing, trusting that it'll come, and singing God's praises day in and day out. Their default setting for suffering is not despairing unbelief. Instead, their faith is instinctive and heartfelt and hopeful. When I visit with my sweet girl Mary (name changed), she tells me about her malaria and asks for prayer. (Mary is eighteen and brilliant and hilarious. I've called her "sweet girl" so many times that in one of her last letters, she called herself "sweet girl.") I clumsily pray for her, secretly wondering if God will do anything, but Mary trusts that he'll show up and answer our prayers. I guess my faith is strengthened when I realize God listened to this girl asking for help with school and sickness and he plucked me out of my minivan and sent me to her village to become her sponsor and do something about it.

After years of growing up in the western Christian world, I had become a little calloused, a little cynical. I went through the motions but didn't always believe that God would provide. Maybe if I worked hard enough, at least he wouldn't get in my way. Getting to know this community in northern Uganda, I discovered friends who prayed because they had no alternative. They believed God would provide because he is God and not because they could force his hand. I saw their faith and I saw their joy in things I take for granted. I had a house filled with things, but they had more than I did. My water came out of a little lever on my sink, and I had electricity at the flick of a plastic switch. And they saw God move with their own eyes. We needed each other.

They taught me it's okay to ask for help. The first time I traveled to northern Uganda to work with HopeChest, I hoped I could "help" this community with its large population of orphaned and vulnerable children. It's funny to me now, thinking back. We think we're going to help *them*, but they end up helping *us*. Isn't that so often the case? And we realize there isn't *them* and *us*, only *we*. I quickly learned that they had some things I needed badly: Unwavering faith in a God who provides. Unblemished joy in the provision of clean water and food. Unimpeded hope in the opportunity to work to provide for themselves. Life was completely unfair. Things were hard, harder than we can imagine, yet they had the faith, joy, and hope that God would heal their community.

At first, I thought I was going to help *them* with *their* poverty problem. But then when I met them, I realized I had a poverty problem too. As I worked to mobilize my community here to come together and partner with our friends in Uganda, we've all worked on projects together, and God has healed our relational and spiritual poverty. As they've developed their community's resources, God has healed their material poverty. We in both communities have empowered one another to pull ourselves out of our poverty. We've helped each other, and that's the way the world should be.

They've taught me about generosity. There's nothing more humbling than to receive a letter in the mail from the child you sponsor and read that she's praying for you. And when we visit, they're lavish in their gifts, giving groundnuts and chickens. I've learned to be generous to visitors, gracious to people who offer gifts. When I attended their Anglican church on my third visit, the minister preached on Hebrews 13:2: "Do not forget to show hospitality to strangers, for by so doing some people have shown hospitality to angels without knowing it." We were no angels, but they took care of us anyway, and I sure hope they got oodles of heavenly credit for doing it.

They taught me about gratitude. One summer when I visited the kids in Uganda, they all asked for mattresses. They were sleeping on the ground and desired some padding and protection for their bodies. On that same visit, we saw the new latrines with their shiny orange paint and the gardens beginning to grow and the oxen plowing a nearby field. New growth and change whistled through the African air and it smelled of promise and hope and fresh grass.

That fall, we heard the devastating news that massive flooding had overtaken the CarePoint area. The latrines were in danger of backing up, the gardens were wiped out, and the risk of waterborne disease threatened the ones we loved. We organized a campaign to raise money for mosquito nets and water-purifying tablets to keep the kids safe from the increased risk of disease. And mattresses. Each child received a new mattress.

When we got the pictures of the flooded fields, the dirty standing water, and the ruined crops, we also got a picture of our group of kids, smiling from ear to ear, holding their new mattresses. In the midst of a really bad situation, they were rejoicing for answered prayer—in the form of the mattresses they'd needed all along.

My Hero

My hero is a sixteen-year-old boy in northern Uganda. I've been his sponsor for six years now, and he has changed my life. So far I've visited him three times and Alex has visited him twice, and he's always really quiet. It's completely awkward when you have the whole village sitting around you and you're speaking through a translator even though his English rocks. But what teen boy wants to practice his language skills in front of his *mzungu* sponsor, his mom, and his whole freaking village?

I was going to write about him, tell his story, but then last month I opened the HopeChest newsletter produced by the Ugandan staff and found that Samuel (name changed) had written his own story. With his permission, I'm sharing it here.

Samuel's Story: They Thought I Was Bewitched

I don't know my father. Nor do I know whether he is dead or alive. I live with my mother and other six children in the internally displaced people's camp. I was born on Christmas day, 25th December 1998. In 2005, when I was in Primary 2, my left leg became infected and developed swellings which burst with smelly pus oozing to form painful wounds. For four years I could not walk well, nor could I go to school. The smell was so unbearable that even my mum would not want to share a room with me at night. She would chase me out of the hut. Even neighbors would not allow me into their houses. I slept out on verandas. Each time I managed to walk to school the class teacher and children would not allow me into the classroom because of the smell. The village people believed that I was bewitched and could not be cured. Everybody feared to have anything to do with my leg or get any help for me because they believed the witchcraft would follow them too. My mother struggled to take me to various hospitals, including visiting traditional healers who used local herbs. All these zeroed to one thing; my leg was to be cut off, but my mother did not have Sh.200,000 (US $80) that the doctors needed for the operation.

It took several months of looking for this money, and in the process HopeChest staff visited the village. My mum explained my situation to the staff, asking them to provide her with the money so that she could take me to hospital to have my leg amputated. When the staff saw me, they decided to pay and take me to a better hospital to see if my leg could be saved.

The doctor clearly said my mum had delayed with me because the infection was so bad that the leg would not be saved.

The HopeChest staff insisted to the doctor to try to save the leg, and if it did not work then it would be amputated. HopeChest paid all the treatment bills, transport, and upkeep in the hospital for one month. I am told over 5 million shillings were spent. My leg improved and I began to go to school. I am now in Primary 7. I am studying hard so I can get good employment in future. I want to be a doctor because I was cured by a doctor.

—*Samuel*

A Sponsor's Story

While Samuel was living that out in Uganda, I was writing this side of the story over here in the US:

Via Unexpected.org
December 13, 2009

So then one day about a month ago, I see a boy's face on my computer screen. He's about twelve. He lives in Uganda and has a cut on his leg that's gotten infected and now threatens his life. I see his face, and then my eyes slide to his leg, and all I can think is "Why?" Why is that his life and this is our life?

When I think about the problem—the atrocity—of extreme poverty, it feels unsolvable. Too big, too late, too much, too painful, too bad. What I do doesn't matter, right? Mmm.

It sure matters to Samuel. What I can do matters to this boy who doesn't live here. He lives there, and he needs ME. And he needs me NOW. My stopping to mull it over, back-burner it, compare it to the hundred other opportunities to give would sentence him to death. He could not survive my putting him on hold.

Samuel desperately needed money to have his leg amputated to save his life. We got involved, started tweeting about the situation, and throughout the day we watched as God brought in the amount needed, with enough extra to feed his family and help with his recovery. What an incredible day to watch God move through people to save this one special boy. About a week later, we found out that he's in the hospital on antibiotics, and the doctors think they may be able to save his leg. Our God is so good.

I don't know why, but I love this boy. And today my friends found his sponsorship packet and let me sponsor him. Alex and I get to sponsor this boy. Now we can write to him about how much God loves him, now I know that our monthly sponsorship is getting him the food he needs, now an educator can teach him to read. I wish I could hug him right now, but now I can hug him this spring when we visit Uganda.

That spring I met Samuel for the first time, held his baby brother who was recovering from malaria, and visited with his mom. We've exchanged letters and photos over the years, and one of my favorite squeal-worthy moments was when we received photos of Samuel playing soccer on his newly healed leg.

And then we got this update from him:

Dear Alex

Hello sponsor! I am happy for the letter I received; it contained some pictures on it was really nice for me to see those pictures.

In fact dad! I read the letter and it was interesting I am also serious in my studies since we started a new term soon at last year from my last term i.e term three I managed to pass p. 5 where I become number 1st to pass and I was the best boy from the whole school and I won a goat given by the project. [HopeChest]

I know Jesus loves me and you as well. I have lots of prayers for you Melanie, Alex, Elliott, Evelyn. God bless you!!!

> *Greeting*
> *from Samuel.*
> *Mum, Simon and all*
> *My brothers in Jesus name Amen!!!*

I've spent time thinking about the last six years and all the incredible moments, from the miraculous to the mundane. How do a couple of ordinary people end up falling in love with a community halfway around the world?

The very first child we sponsored in Uganda started a domino effect that has impacted thousands of orphaned and vulnerable children there and sponsors and donors here. This extraordinary boy's story jump-started the whole unexpected thing.

I can't get over a God who cares so much about one life, one leg. He brought us together across the world.

Samuel's life, what happened to him, wasn't fair. But that's not stopping him one tiny bit. His story strengthens my faith, brings me hope, and gives me determination to not let my circumstances stand in the way of embracing the life God has for me. He's inspired countless people in the US who have heard his story, and hundreds if not thousands of children have been sponsored because of Samuel's story of partnership and hope.

Empowered to Help

Life isn't fair. It's not fair for kids to sleep on the wet ground and have their crops wiped out by floods and have malaria and have their legs infected, and . . . I know you could fill in a hundred more unfairnesses right here if I gave you the space.

Why does God allow bad things to happen? Smarter people than I continue to wrestle with this question.

What's my part of the solution? Now that's a question we can wrap our brains around. What's your part of the solution? Whatever's going on in your heart or whatever issue you can't shake out of your head . . . how can you help? What's a first step? Is it learning more about a situation on the web, asking people from a local organization what they need, sponsoring a child and beginning that relationship, calling your local school to get more involved? Is it learning more about foster care, taking a meal to a friend who had surgery, supporting a ministry that helps marginalized women find employment? Maybe it's something right in your own family.

I don't know why God lets awful stuff happen. Let's all ask him. Ask him as often as you like. Wrestle it out with him. But in your wrestling, in the wondering, what's our part of the solution? How can we make the bad things better? While we're asking him why he allows it, let's ask him what we should do to fix it.

When God breaks our heart for the injustice of others, he positions us as his hands and feet. We move from feeling victimized and powerless to feeling empowered to help.

Via Twitter @UnexpectedMel

Elliott: The car is getting messy again.

Me: Why don't we take the trash out with us when we get out of the car today?

Elliott: Good idea. Why don't you do it since it was your plan?

Failure, Doubt, and Being Bananaballs

Claire Colburn: So you failed. All right you really failed. You failed. You failed. You failed. You failed. You failed. You failed. You failed. You failed. You failed. You failed. You failed. You failed. You think I care about that? I do understand. You wanna be really great? Then have the courage to fail big and stick around. Make them wonder why you're still smiling.

—*Elizabethtown*[1]

After I experienced peace with infertility, and adoption became Plan A and exactly what I wanted and longed for, a few years into the new plan, I experienced a new kind of doubt, a severely sea-sick-inducing rocking of my faith. I didn't doubt God, but I doubted my ability to hear him.

When we brought Evie home, we went through a major adjustment period, going from one to two kids, helping her through major health and emotional hurdles, and dealing with my own selfishness and impatience.

That last part completely surprised me. Apparently I had an inflated view of my own capacity for longsuffering. How could I be impatient with my children? I waited waaay longer than the usual allotted time to acquire them. I should be filled with patience, ridiculously selfless, and fully capable of handling all the things. I was not. If you have kids, you might know what I mean, when their needs outweigh your ability to respond with poise and grace, and you end up spending more time than you'd like to admit locked in the bathroom by yourself.

I still greet my utter depravity every morning with a friendly wave and nod of determination. "I see you, Utter Depravity. You won't go away, but I'll keep gripping the kitchen counter, asking forgiveness for my harried inner monster, and begging God to help me not ruin my kids."

Anyway, even in the midst of adjusting to our family of four, we still felt the same incompleteness we felt when we were three. Team Dale wasn't done, and we weren't sure what was next, but we figured we'd listen to God, be available, and keep our eyes open.

Then we experienced five "failed" possible adoptions in a row. I say failed with li'l quote marks, because while they felt like failures to us, they were exactly the right thing for each child. So while I licked my wounds and felt totally adrift, the most important people, the kids, were right where they should be. I'm an adult. I can take it. Where's that fuzzy blanket?!

From a local infant adoption to international older child adoptions, things just kept falling apart, and at the end of our two-year spree of nothingness, I felt like we were crazy headless chickens running around whenever we heard God whisper in the wind. I had thought we were rational, thoughtful people, but apparently I could not discern God's voice from a neon picture on a Lite-Brite.

I love what Preston Yancey says in *Tables in the Wilderness*:

> You look around and see all the shiny, happy people who seem to be hearing God through every little brush of wind and flap of butterfly wings and wonder if everyone is crazy and you're the only one who is sane or—worse—you're the only crazy one and everyone else is sane.[2]

Was I hearing butterflies? Was I completely bananaballs? I unsubscribed from all the adoption blogs and deleted emails and stopped trying so hard. I worried that this whole thing had been smoke and mirrors and God had never really led us anywhere.

Hot Pink Sweater

And then one day this smiling girl in a hot pink sweater with her hands on her hips appeared in my inbox.

I deleted the email immediately. I was done. Everything was a lie. I couldn't hear God, and he probably didn't care what I did.

Weeks went by, and I focused on the two littles in front of me and confronted the sad reality that I was not in fact the savior of all the children in the world and in fact they would all get along fine without me.

And then one day that same dang photo showed up back in my inbox. The sender said if she didn't hear back, she wouldn't bug me again. This was her last attempt. Dang it. I clicked on the picture.

I still don't fully understand how to listen for and hear from God. I'm no longer 100 percent sure about that. All I know is that the little girl in the hot pink sweater calls me Mom and rolls her eyes at me and throws her arms around my waist.

Sometimes God works even through our doubt, whether we're doubting him or doubting ourselves. Sometimes I guess we just have to open an email.

And really, thinking back on our five "failures," God used each one of them to bring our hearts to exactly where we needed to be for Ana. They weren't failures at all. They were my own stumbling steps as a toddler learning to walk toward her parent.

Via Unexpected.org
December 1, 2010

Blah. Surrender is following me around. Apparently I'm so completely not in control of my life. I seem to remember this fact . . . and yet I render surprise all over again when confronted with the need to surrender what already isn't mine. Ahem. Yep.

Sigh. My prayers are not artfully crafted. This past year I've gone from bumbling prayers to wordy prayers to small prayers for big things. Just *God I surrender. God show up show me show Yourself show. Lead me. I surrender. Help me to hear you.*

The older and "wiser" I get, the more helpless I feel. I know that's a good thing. I feel like Elliott as a tiny preemie, when I'd put him on his tummy and he couldn't even lift his head. He was completely at my mercy. If he was facing a wall, he faced that wall until I turned his head. He was floppy and completely incapable of doing anything but passively surrendering his life to me. All he could do was cry. Ah. Yes. That's it. He could cry. That's where I'm headed. That's where I'm getting, that place where I'm completely helpless and all I can do is cry to my Father to move me. To come to my rescue.

These aren't sad tears or bad tears or mopey tears. These are tears of surrender. They're beautiful. I hope—I pray—that over the next several months—some of the craziest months I've ever had, I think—I will learn the beauty of surrender. I'm showing up. I'm here. Now I'm crying out to my Father to turn my head so I'll see what he wants me to see.

Everything Will Be Okay If . . .

Kevin: What's the worst thing that can happen? We'll all die, right?
—*Space Camp*[1]

I would be fine if I could just get pregnant. I would be fine if Elliott could just come home from the hospital. I would be fine if we could have a bigger family. I would be fine if the adoptions came through. I would be fine if we could get the right diagnosis . . .

Have you ever played this game with yourself? Everything will be okay if . . .

I make it to summer.
He just leaves her.
The tumor is benign.
I can just get this job.
I can just get pregnant.

We all have these thoughts, but if you're like me, sometimes you can live your life holding your breath for the next thing. If I can just get here, or if this will just happen, or as long as they do this . . . everything will be okay. As I mentioned before, I spent most of my twenties *iffing* my life away.

Why Does Life Have to Be So Hard?

My oldest (and newest) daughter, Ana, is upbeat and energetic most of the time. Early in the morning, late at night, she invented perky. And she's gone through more in her ten little years than

197

most people would experience in ten lifetimes. Maybe someday she'll write a book of her own, but for now, she's given me permission to share this story from a few nights ago.

Last year, at nine years old, Ana made a choice, a choice that's too big for a nine-year-old, but one she had to make anyway. The court presented her with the option for us to adopt her, to live in a family that loves her, to have a permanent, stable home. The price was leaving her country and language and culture and the people she knew. She made the choice and she's entered her new life with gusto and unbelievable courage and tenacity.

And last week I heard her crying late at night at the top of the stairs. Her face appeared over the railing, and she asked about a close friend from Latvia. She was grieving because she had forgotten her for a time. How could she forget her friend? The enormity of the loss of her friend, her culture, her language—which try as she might is slipping as she works on English at school and home—engulfed her and she dissolved into my arms in sobs.

She cried, "Why does my life have to be so hard?"

"I don't know, precious, I don't know," I whispered back, stroking her hair. "I'm so grateful to be your second mom, but I wish you never had to lose your first mom. I'm so sorry. I wish I could make it all better."

This is a snapshot of adoption, comforting the child you love and wishing she could be comforted by her first mom. This is adoption, sobbing into your new mom's T-shirt as you grieve the loss of your first family. We're both broken and clinging to each other and wishing we could fix it.

Why does life have to be so hard? When will it be okay?

Most of the time, there are no easy answers.

When we feel out of control, careening through the air toward Vulcan without parachutes like Kirk and Sulu, we create scenarios in our minds in which it'll all turn out right, and we'll get beamed back to the *Enterprise* in the nick of time before SPLAT.

The careening makes us feel helpless.

Via Unexpected.org
October 8, 2010

Dear God, hi. I really want to pick up the phone and start calling my people, but I need to shoot this your way . . . but my brain is too swampy to just think at you, so I'm blogging at you. You know, I've been pretty fine with the waiting for a referral. But now I'm a little past the "average" wait time, and even though I know it's just an average, I'm still getting really antsy. I'm sitting here weepy, and there's throat lumpiness. I'm so aware of my lack of control. I have decisions to make for the future, and I can't even see tomorrow. Help! I need some serious wisdom right now. What's headed our way? Who's headed our way? When? Give me the strength to invest in TODAY. I kinda just want to have all my people over for a big sleepover and drink coffee and stay in my jammies until I get the call. Breathe. Surrender.

Is God Enough?

There's always something that could be better in my life, and for the most part, I've learned to enjoy life even in the midst of the pain. (See chapter 13, "Count the Wins (Even While You're Losing)," if you need a refresher about the New Yorkiness.) But the question I began asking myself, as prayers were answered and as new challenges arose, was: When will I have enough?

Is God enough?
If I never have a baby, is he enough?
If I lose that baby, is he enough?
If the adoption doesn't come through, is he enough?
If my precious child suffers, is God enough?
Maybe you've asked yourself that question too.
Is God enough?

If you never get married, is he enough?

If you never land your dream job, is he enough?

If you suffer from mental or physical pain, is he enough?

If you've lost your dearest person, is God enough?

Honestly, your answer doesn't have to be yes. It doesn't have to be. Ask yourself if God is enough, and be brave enough not to censor your answer. Don't play games. It's in your own head. Is he enough? If he is, why do you believe that? If you don't think he's enough, admit that to yourself and ask why. It's better to be honest with yourself than to go through the motions.

And once you're honest with yourself, then you can find the freedom to be honest with God. Tell him you don't think he's enough. You can ask him to change your mind, or you can just tell him and let it hang there for a while.

Marinate there for a bit. What is enough? When you've lost something huge—a person, a job, a dream—what is enough? Who is enough?

For me, I finally had to admit to myself that there's no such thing as *enough*. I always want more, I love change, and I'm always straining to the next thing. Contentment is a unicorn. I'm like my child who, the day after Christmas, came up to me and asked, "Are there more presents? I want more."

Well. I appreciated the honesty. "No, honey, the North Pole burned down. Now walk away and let Mommy drink her coffee." What. I would *never*.

Kristy's Story: I Wanted to Give Up

I married my high school sweetheart. We attended college and waited a few years to try to have children. Once we deemed it "safe" to get pregnant, pregnancy didn't come easily. We prayed and waited what seemed like a long time. Then we got pregnant! I just knew that God had answered our prayers and had blessed us with this pregnancy. We planned cutesy ways to tell our family that we were expecting.

Our parents were so excited, enthralled at the idea that we were going to make them grandparents!

A few weeks later, I lost the pregnancy.

I was blindsided. I was heartbroken.

I knew that things like that could happen, but never imagined it would happen to me. I didn't understand how I could have problems with pregnancy when no one else in my family had a history of that sort. We mourned, we cried, we screamed, and asked "Why?!" The doctor told us we had to wait three months to try again, and to our surprise, we got pregnant immediately after the prescribed three months.

We were PREGNANT! Glory be to God! He'd obviously been testing us, disciplining us, or teaching us something during the first pregnancy and loss. We were so grateful for the trial before, as it made us appreciate this pregnancy that much more. I was sure that I'd "seen the light" at the end of the tunnel and God had led us through it to get to where I was.

A few weeks later, I lost the second pregnancy.

How could God do this to me? To us?

Had we not been faithful in our prayers? Had we not believed and trusted and obeyed? I thought, "God, why? Why me? Why don't you love me?" My heart went into a dark place for a while. I allowed negative and evil thoughts to seep into my mind. I felt like my world was spiraling out of control. I didn't understand. I considered suicide. I thought that my husband would be better without me, better with someone who could give him children. I was wrong.

I wanted to give up.

I didn't want to try to have children again, and I thought that God might be showing me a different path, a life without children filled with a different adventure. I clung to God. Someone once told me, "Jesus will never be all that you need, until Jesus is all that you have." In that time, aside from the loving support of my husband and our family, all I had was Jesus. My hope, my plans, and my future I felt were very dim. I held tightly to God and prayed that he would remove the desire to have children from my heart if I wasn't able to have them.

My sister had a friend who had experienced infertility and recommended that I talk with her. I messaged the friend (yep, a total stranger) and let my story and tears flow. It was the first time I'd talked to someone who'd experienced infertility and could really understand my pain. I realized immediately we aren't meant to endure struggles alone. Finding someone who gets it really does make a huge difference. The listening ear of someone who endured the same trials made me capable of being that person to others. If you haven't experienced infertility, there's no way to really know how to respond.

—*Kristy B.*

Big Questions That Are Way Too Big for Me

You followed all the rules, but still, everything fell apart. You're hurt and angry, and deep down, there's a twinge of something scarier, something hard to admit. Is God trustworthy? How do we reconcile a loving God with our wreckage? How can we rely on a God we aren't sure we can trust with our dreams? I have these big questions that are way too big for me to answer.

When something horrible happens, people want to know why.

They ask you questions and try to figure out why the bad thing happened to you, and why it won't happen to them. Oh, he got cancer because smoking, because genetics, because bad moral choice, because metabolism, neighborhood, or experimental drug.

We do this too, try to find the blame. I went on a huge environmental kick, getting rid of any toxin that is possibly known to cause infertility. I secretly feared the scary drug I took for acne in high school caused it. I blamed myself for narcissism, exchanging a baby for clear skin.

Solution-finding isn't bad. It's good to try to pinpoint the problem, and if there's anything in our lives that we need to adjust or own up to or fix, then yes, by all means, let's tinker with all that and do our part.

But sometimes there isn't anything on this earth to blame. Sometimes these things are above our pay grades. Sometimes we blame God, the ultimate blame-receiver. And he's God, so he can take it.

If God is our heavenly Father, he really does parent his kids differently. My kids get mad when they find out I took one for ice cream after a doctor's appointment. "It's not fair," they grumble, and how much more so do we experience that as God's children? "You gave her a baby and I didn't get one." "You gave him a house and I don't have one." "You gave me free education and running water and they have to walk miles for their water and miss school to get it." We blame God for the unfairness.

> **Via Twitter @UnexpectedMel**
>
> When I stopped trying to be a good Christian and started being Melanie, created and loved by God, everything changed.

Okay, so if kids can be completely honest and scream about fairness and injustice and trust and anger over ice cream and chore charts, maybe in our own journeys, in our own way, we need to do the same. Admit some stuff out loud.

"Everything is not okay."

"Honestly, I don't think I trust God completely even though

I'm going through the motions so people don't freak out on me and I don't freak out on myself, because if I admit that I feel this way, I step into this very grayish *Matrix-y* world, and I'm not sure I'll ever figure out how to get out."

"I don't know if God loves me, because this doesn't feel loving."

"It's not fair."

A Bunch of Bible Stuff for All Your Various Moods

> Shepherd Book: River, you don't . . . fix the Bible.
>
> River: It's broken. It doesn't make sense.
>
> Shepherd Book: It's not about . . . making sense. It's about believing in something. And letting that belief be real enough to change your life. It's about faith. You don't fix faith, River. It fixes you.
>
> —*Firefly*[1]

I don't know what it is about hard times that make me want to crack open my Bible more often, but it's one of the things I actually appreciate about life's proverbial valleys. I read with a pen in my hand and in the margins write whatever I'm feeling, uncensored. Over the years I can go back through the pages and see the words that hit me, encouraged me, confused me, or angered me. The Bible is interactive. It isn't meant to sit prissily on a shelf. It's meant to be consumed, screamed at, cried on, and hugged.

At times I've tried to ignore the Bible, but I keep coming back to it, day after day, year after year. The words inside are like family. They're raw and awkward and offensive and loving and encouraging and hopeful.

The Bible is also useful for those times when I just don't have the words. Sometimes I think, "I'm old and tired and I got nothin'. I'm out of words. I don't have the energy to think of what to say to God." Time with God starts to feel like a bad date when you stare awkwardly at each other and twist your napkin with your hands.

When times are tough and the hard questions are swirling in your brain and grief and pain are gripping your heart, repeat God's words back to him. Say them in your head. Say them out loud. I'm not saying claim these words like they're promises for you specifically. I don't really go in for the idea of claiming words for myself, like I run across something in the Bible and shout, "Mine!" enthusiastically. These words were written by other people during specific times, and I don't necessarily think that because God did something one way then he's going to do it the same way for me. He's never given me a bunch of acres of land or asked me to defeat the Midianites. However, I find great comfort and inspiration in these words that are preserved for us through the centuries. They reveal God's character and his interactions with people just like us. And so I connect into a faith lineage that is longer and larger than myself, and I find hope and encouragement from his very presence in the lives of real people through the ages. And I write really intellectual stuff in the margins of my Bible, like "whoa" and "dude."

In *Undaunted*, Christine Caine says, "When there is a fight between your heart and your head, experience has taught me that the best thing to do is pick up your Bible and remind yourself of what God says."[2]

Here are some of my favorite passages for when you're going through something hard, compiled into lists based on how you're feeling. And I mean, if you just really need a good Bible bidet of encouragement and go-forth-iness, sit on the whole of Romans 8.

Sometimes things are so bad that you can't even talk about them with God. Maybe you don't know where to begin. Maybe you're fairly certain he isn't even there and definitely isn't listening. Maybe you don't want to say the thing out loud because then it's true. When I get like that, I say that. "God, there's something I need to talk about, but I don't want to talk about it."

Do that for a few days or however long. Then maybe move

up to "God, here's the thing _____. But I'm not talking about it." Just say it out loud, even if you worry you might be talking to yourself and you're finally having that break with reality you were worried about. When you're hurting, it's okay to do crazy things, like talk to a God you aren't sure you believe in about something you aren't ready to admit out loud. Totally okay.

Or maybe you really, really believe and you're heartbroken that the God you've devoted your whole freaking life to isn't answering. That he's definitely not fair, and he's not playing by the rules that you made up for him in your head. I get that. Blerg, do I ever get that. So just read the words back to him, the ones he left for us in the first place. And tears count as prayer. And sighs. And groans. It all counts. You don't have to form actual words. You can just sit in his presence and groan at him. I've been doing that for years.

When You Want to Shred Something with Your Bare Hands

How long, LORD, must I call for help,
    but you do not listen?
Or cry out to you, "Violence!"
    but you do not save?
Why do you make me look at injustice?
    Why do you tolerate wrongdoing?
Destruction and violence are before me;
    there is strife, and conflict abounds.
Therefore the law is paralyzed,
    and justice never prevails.
The wicked hem in the righteous,
    so that justice is perverted.

Habakkuk 1:2–4

Do not take revenge, my friends, but leave room for God's wrath, for it is written: "It is mine to avenge; I will repay," says the Lord. Romans 12:19

I cried out to God for help;
  I cried out to God to hear me.
When I was in distress, I sought the Lord;
    at night I stretched out untiring hands,
    and I would not be comforted.
I remembered you, God, and I groaned;
    I meditated, and my spirit grew faint.
"Will the Lord reject forever?
    Will he never show his favor again?
Has his unfailing love vanished forever?
    Has his promise failed for all time?
Has God forgotten to be merciful?
    Has he in anger withheld his compassion?"
"I will remember the deeds of the LORD;
    yes, I will remember your miracles of long ago.
I will consider all your works
    and meditate on all your mighty deeds."

Psalm 77:1–3, 7–9, 11–12

Via Unexpected.org
June 14, 2011

Today I picked up Isaiah, and chapters 41–43 just about laid me flat. Over and over, God talks about holding our hand, upholding us with his hand, hand hand hand. Such cool imagery. I literally squeezed my hand in a ball as if squeezing his hand back. Whoa. And it just hit me. In chapter 41, he talks about holding our right hand, and he talks about upholding us with his righteous right hand. So . . . does that mean he's facing us? He's not standing next to us holding our right hand with his left hand. He's facing us like a handshake? I don't know . . . but it feels so strong to me, no flaccid, limp hand from God. Nope. Strong, holding me up, gripping me with his hand!

In chapter 42, he describes himself both as a mighty man and a warrior . . . AND like a woman in childbirth!!! My God fights for us as a man, a warrior, a woman. And how cool to find a laboring woman with imagery of a WARRIOR!

When You Want to Pull the Blanket Over Your Head

The LORD is my rock, my fortress and my deliverer;
> my God is my rock, in whom I take refuge.
> my shield and the horn of my salvation, my stronghold.
In my distress I called to the LORD;
> I cried to my God for help.
From his temple he heard my voice;
> my cry came before him, into his ears.

Psalm 18:2, 6

But he said to me, "My grace is sufficient for you, for my power is made perfect in weakness." Therefore I will boast all the more gladly about my weaknesses, so that Christ's power may rest on me. That is why, for Christ's sake, I delight in weaknesses, in insults, in hardships, in persecutions, in difficulties. For when I am weak, then I am strong. 2 Corinthians 12:9–10

You are my hiding place;
> you will protect me from trouble
> and surround me with songs of deliverance.
I will instruct you and teach you in the way you should go;
> I will counsel you with my loving eye on you.

Psalm 32:7–8

"Have I not commanded you? Be strong and courageous! Do not be afraid; do not be discouraged, for the LORD your God will be with you wherever you go." Joshua 1:9

"I will repay you for the years the locusts have eaten." Joel 2:25

"The LORD your God is with you,
    the Mighty Warrior who saves.
He will take great delight in you;
    in his love he will no longer rebuke you,
    but will rejoice over you with singing."

Zephaniah 3:17

For I am convinced that neither death nor life, neither angels nor demons, neither the present nor the future, nor any powers, neither height nor depth, nor anything else in all creation, will be able to separate us from the love of God that is in Christ Jesus our Lord. Romans 8:38–39

Psalm 91. The whole thing.

When You're Feeling Upbeat and Full of Hopefulness

May the God of hope fill you with all joy and peace as you trust in him, so that you may overflow with hope by the power of the Holy Spirit. Romans 15:13

I keep asking that the God of our Lord Jesus Christ, the glorious Father, may give you the Spirit of wisdom and revelation, so that you may know him better. I pray that the eyes of your heart may be enlightened in order that you may know the hope to which he has called you, the riches of his glorious inheritance in his holy people, and his incomparably great power for us who believe. Ephesians 1:17–19

With your help I can advance against a troop;
    with my God I can scale a wall.
You make your saving help my shield,
    and your right hand sustains me;
    your help has made me great.
You provide a broad path for my feet,
    so that my ankles do not give way.

Psalm 18:29, 35–36

I have learned the secret of being content in any and every situation, whether well fed or hungry, whether living in plenty or in want. I can do all this through him who gives me strength. Philippians 4:12–13

Hear my cry for help,
    my King and my God,
    for to you I pray.
In the morning, LORD, you hear my voice;
    in the morning I lay my requests before you
    and wait expectantly.

Psalm 5:2–3

Because of the LORD's great love we are not consumed,
    for his compassions never fail.
They are new every morning;
    great is your faithfulness.

Lamentations 3:22–23

Not only so, but we also glory in our sufferings, because we know that suffering produces perseverance; perseverance, character; and character, hope. And hope does not put us to shame, because God's love has been poured out into our hearts through the Holy Spirit, who has been given to us. Romans 5:3–5

When You're Feeling Despondent and "My Dead Puppy"

> Though the fig tree does not bud
> and there are no grapes on the vines,
> though the olive crop fails
> and the fields produce no food,
> though there are no sheep in the pen
> and no cattle in the stalls,
> yet I will rejoice in the LORD,
> I will be joyful in God my Savior.
> The Sovereign LORD is my strength;
> he makes my feet like the feet of a deer,
> he enables me to tread on the heights.
>
> *Habakkuk 3:17–19*

I pray that you, being rooted and established in love, may have power, together with all the Lord's holy people, to grasp how wide and long and high and deep is the love of Christ, and to know this love that surpasses knowledge—that you may be filled to the measure of all the fullness of God. Now to him who is able to do immeasurably more than all we ask or imagine, according to his power that is at work within us, to him be glory in the church and in Christ Jesus throughout all generations, for ever and ever! Amen. Ephesians 3:17–21

Being confident of this, that he who began a good work in you will carry it on to completion until the day of Christ Jesus. Philippians 1:6

> Why, my soul, are you downcast?
> Why so disturbed within me?
> Put your hope in God,
> for I will yet praise him,
> my Savior and my God.
>
> *Psalm 43:5*

I am feeble and utterly crushed;
    I groan in anguish of heart.
All my longings lie open before you, Lord;
    my sighing is not hidden from you.
Come quickly to help me,
    my Lord and my Savior.

Psalm 38:8–9, 22

I will praise the LORD, who counsels me;
    even at night my heart instructs me.
I keep my eyes always on the LORD.
    With him at my right hand, I will not be shaken.

Psalm 16:7–8

"Peace I leave with you; my peace I give you. I do not give to you as the world gives. Do not let your hearts be troubled and do not be afraid." John 14:27

Therefore we do not lose heart. Though outwardly we are wasting away, yet inwardly we are being renewed day by day. For our light and momentary troubles are achieving for us an eternal glory that far outweighs them all. So we fix our eyes not on what is seen, but on what is unseen, since what is seen is temporary, but what is unseen is eternal. 2 Corinthians 4:16–18

When You Feel Like You Need to Remind God About Some Stuff

Hope deferred makes the heart sick,
    but a longing fulfilled is a tree of life.

Proverbs 13:12

And we know that in all things God works for the good of those who love him, who have been called according to his purpose. What, then, shall we say in response to these things? If God is for us, who can be against us? Romans 8:28, 31

For the LORD your God is a merciful God; he will not abandon or destroy you. Deuteronomy 4:31

"Pardon me, my lord," Gideon replied, "but if the LORD is with us, why has all this happened to us? Where are all his wonders that our ancestors told us about when they said, 'Did not the LORD bring us up out of Egypt?' But now the LORD has abandoned us and put us into the hand of Midian." Judges 6:13

"Ask and it will be given to you; seek and you will find; knock and the door will be opened to you. For everyone who asks receives; the one who seeks finds; and to the one who knocks, the door will be opened. Which of you, if your son asks for bread, will give him a stone? Or if he asks for a fish, will give him a snake? If you, then, though you are evil, know how to give good gifts to your children, how much more will your Father in heaven give good gifts to those who ask him!" Matthew 7:7–11

Listen to me, you descendants of Jacob,
　　all the remnant of the people of Israel,
you whom I have upheld since your birth,
　　and have carried since you were born.
Even to your old age and gray hairs
　　I am he, I am he who will sustain you.
I have made you and I will carry you;
　　I will sustain you and I will rescue you.
I say, "My purpose will stand,
　　and I will do all that I please."
From the east I summon a bird of prey;
　　from a far-off land, a man to fulfill my purpose.
What I have said, that will I bring about;
　　what I have planned, that will I do.

Isaiah 46:3–4, 10–11

-PART-
SIX

What's Next?

*You've Felt the Feelings, Employed
Various Coping Mechanisms, Asked the
Hard Questions . . . So Now What?*

How to Survive the Death of a Dream

> Samantha James: I love it that you're taking me home to meet your mom. Was this one of your clever little plans?
>
> Chris: Yes. I planned you setting the plane on fire.
>
> —*Just Friends*[1]

The cries of "It's not fair!" rise so loudly around our house that the kids even cry foul over good things. Last year, all of us had a horrific, boogery cold and cough. We were drowning in our own phlegm (Would you like me to describe it further?!?), and I was passing out children's Mucinex like it was water. Evie was the only healthy one of us, and she was angry about it. "Aww! It's not fair! Everyone gets to be sick but me!" I tried to explain to her that health was a *good* thing, but reasoning with a four-year-old determined to whine is like trying to tell a grown man he can't have an iPhone.

Britt's Story: The Fair

When my kids tell me it's not fair, I tell them, "You're right. Fair comes once a year. August." (As in The Fair. My kids do not see the humor. But they do stop whining about it being fair!)

—*Britt P.*

Sometimes I'm like Evie, and focusing on what everyone else has clouds my ability to see what I have right in front of me. After

217

losing my in vitro freezer babies in both the longest and shortest miscarriage imaginable (freezer time: two years; uterus time: two weeks), I went to counseling for sadness. I just couldn't stop being sad, and it was choking out my ability to love the life I already had.

When I thawed out my freezer babies and they squirted them up inside me with the giant turkey baster, I felt good. This had worked before. Over the next couple of weeks, I felt changes similar to the first time, so I ventured into hope and told our families I was pretty sure I was pregnant. On test result day, Mom came over to wait with me, and we watched *The Last Holiday*, and I will always have a soft spot for Queen Latifah. Halfway through the movie, about the time she was trying out bungee jumping, I got the call, and Mom paused the movie. The second I heard the nurse's voice on the phone, I knew. I could visualize her with her head cocked to the side and brows furrowed. Pity Face. No babies.

I walked upstairs, told Alex, cried, wiped my eyes, and went back downstairs. Queen Latifah bungeed off that bridge.

Alex and I took a weekend to wallow or heal or rest or whatever and checked into a spa with a fancy room and a vineyard. We needed to drink red wine and walk around in public in our bathrobes and slippers for two days. On the first night, we hadn't been in the hot tub five minutes when a woman joined us and tried to make small talk. "How many kids do you have?"

I escaped back to the room. There wasn't enough wine in the world to make my heart okay. A few weeks later I started counseling, and when she asked why I was there, I said, "I'm sad, and I don't know how to be not sad."

And that's it. Sometimes we just don't know how to be not sad. We have things we can do to dull the sadness or distract us or pretend, but nothing makes it go away. Just time. We need time and we need to face it.

My son was toddling around on new sea legs, and I was sinking further down into those old feelings of depression.

So I didn't know how a counselor could possibly help, and I had weird, guilty thoughts that I could probably work this out myself with just my Bible and prayer, but I went anyway. I went because I was sad, and it's okay to tell people that and ask for help even if you aren't sure how anybody can help, short of fixing your problem by knocking you up with a baby. And Bibles and prayers are great. Also great are people who have gone to school for years and years to learn how to help you work through things.

The counselor made me start journaling again. Each week Dad would watch Elliott while I went to counseling, then I'd go over to his house for my boy and a cup of coffee. I'd rock in the chair on his back porch and say, "I don't know." And I didn't. I didn't know how to get better, but I shuffled my tired feet in the direction I wanted to go. I didn't know how I'd get there, but I turned toward joy, saw it way off in the distance, and shuffled my feet.

With new challenges facing our family as we learn how to parent our beautiful children, I'm shuffling my feet toward joy again. For the last few months, we've been giving things names, winnowing out the descriptions and reasons. Naming things helps us. I'm reminded of Adam, of Garden of Eden fame, and how he named things for God. That was his first job, I think. Official namer. The first job of the first human was Namer. Naming brings relief and naming brings weight.

What do you do when parenting (or marriage, or your career) is different than you thought it would be? You start out with ideas about what you'll do with your kids. If you played sports growing up you dream of sports and coaching your kids and cheering from the sidelines. You dream of Gatorade and oranges. If you were spelling bee champ you picture your child up in front of the school owning the whole dang dictionary. If you had good friends, you imagine hosting pizza parties for happy school friends. You say your kids can be whatever they want to be, but then when you arrive at a place where their options or interests or abilities are different than you pictured . . . you have to sit with that for a moment. Sometimes parenting is different than we plan for. Sometimes we have to lay down all the expectations we didn't even realize we had. We have to grieve a loss before we can celebrate the unexpected blessing.

I'm learning how to enter my kids' worlds and getting excited about what makes them tick. I'm laying down the expectations I had and discovering a brave new path. But it can take a minute. It takes time to accept that you're on a new planet and get out of the spaceship and explore the terrain.

Sometimes we just go through the motions, "fake it till you make it." And that's something. I think it starts at fake and transitions into real as your heart remembers how to beat again. Keep shuffling.

A Part of Us Can't Survive

When dreams die, a part of us dies with them. It has to. A baby, a family, a marriage, a career. A part of us can't survive some of the hardest things life brings. A part of us gets buried in the ground or torn apart in the shredder.

It isn't easy finding yourself again, digging yourself out of the wreckage. I remember telling a new friend in DC when I was struggling through infertility the first time that I wished she could've known me before, back when I was fun. I told her, "I used to be fun. I remember it."

Over the last few years, I've been finding myself again. I think some of the old me died, but some new parts have sprung to life, and I'm discovering that I like myself. It took time, friends, crooning Aerosmith alone, and faith.

> **Via Twitter @UnexpectedMel**
>
> *Evie: We have to get to school I don't know if I'm the line leader I might be the line leader I HAVE TO BE THE LINE LEADER.*
>
> #preschoolpowertrip

In all of it, part of my faith died too. Part of my faith in God is buried in the ground with my dreams for how my life would look. I used to have a chapter and verse for everything. I would look with consternation at people doubting and struggling. God used to fit perfectly in my tidy constructs and everything made sense. Until it didn't.

The other day I admitted to a friend, "I feel like I'm going through a spiritual midlife crisis. And I'm trying to write a book in the middle of it. I wish I'd written it fifteen years ago when everything was incredibly black and white." But maybe, maybe this is exactly when I should be writing down these thoughts about life and unfairness, in the middle of the not knowing. In the middle of my kerfloofiness. I feel like I've let go of one side of the deep end of the pool and swum to the middle. I'm treading water, looking at the side I came from and at the other sides, and I just keep treading, not ready to grab on to any side and feeling myself build endurance and strength as I tread.

I had views and now I have conversations. I made statements and now I ask questions.

My faith is being boiled down to its basic building blocks. I am a work in progress, and Fifteen Years Ago Me would be horrified that I'm not more adamant about things here, and who knows what Fifteen Years From Now Me will think looking back. For whatever reason, I'm writing this book now, where I am, kind of messy and in love with a Savior I don't understand. It is what it is.

My faith is grayer now, and that feels embarrassing to admit out loud, like I've lost gold stars on the Sunday school attendance flannelgraph. I'm learning to find my faith amidst the grays. God is so much bigger and wilder than I ever imagined, and I don't understand and can no longer pretend to quantify his work in the world and in my life.

My faith is grayer and it's also weathered, like a soldier. It's seen battle, and it survived, scarred and shell-shocked but nonetheless alive and present in the world. My faith has stories to tell, and sometimes it gazes off in the distance, remembering the closeness of an untamed Lord. My faith doesn't freak out over the little stuff anymore. It doesn't need to defend anything or rush to strengthen any seeming chink in its armor. It's unarmed and unclothed and unadorned. It just is . . . which seems appropriate for a God who calls himself "I Am."

Naomi's Story: I Will Never Be the Person I Was

I am thirty-two years old.

Two years ago, I left a cult. Two years, two months, and about ten days. I'm not exactly sure on the days, because leaving was a process and there was no real cutoff date—more of a gradual phasing out. First someone asked me a question, and it made me think harder than I had ever thought. I took some time coming up with an answer. Then I realized my answer didn't match the doctrine being taught around me, but the doctrine didn't make sense, and everybody had opinions different than mine. They reacted badly to my opinion, and my critical thinking process came to life a little more. Then, eventually, I left. Different opinions were not tolerated, and friends and family stopped communicating with me, or blamed me, or accused me of a myriad of things, and I realized for sure, 100 percent, that it was a cult.

And I was on the outside.

I was so blessed to have my husband alongside, and we left together with our two children.

In case you think maybe it was just a really strict church and maybe we should have been more gracious or patient, let me put your mind to rest. There were prophets and fear of the end times and dress codes and isolation too. It was a cult.

The only thing is, no one born into a cult immediately thinks it is one. It is secure. It is community. It is safe. Everyone thinks just like you, and you are elite, because you have the extra-special revelation reserved for only a few chosen people, and you can pity the rest of the world for not having it. Never, ever do you expect to have this security fall apart and leave you with barely your own sanity.

I have had a few moments of thinking, "This really isn't fair." It so isn't fair that at thirty years old—this milestone birthday—I was learning to put on mascara and watching YouTube tutorials like a teenager. I trembled in fear at the thought of wearing pants and felt dreadfully awkward in public as I struggled to balance an extreme past with an unknown future. There were some amazing novelties—like the aforesaid mascara and, shall we say, "concealer"—but I had also lost every close friend I had, and my family thought I had committed the unpardonable sin. I dreaded accidentally meeting a member of that church in the grocery store or at the park.

It was as if someone had thrown a bomb into my life. I didn't know how to think, to dress, to study the Bible, to give, to parent, or to make friends. There were so many unwritten rules I had absorbed in my almost thirty years of living, and I acted upon them daily with complete security. Then in one day they were obliterated, and I was left feeling naked, vulnerable, and incredibly socially awkward. I was a walking shell of a person, and no doubt people wondered about that dead look in my eyes a few times. I didn't always come across as super-friendly, and I wasn't. How could I explain the betrayal and rejection I'd felt at the loss of so many friends and family simply for changing doctrine? How could I trust someone again? How could I start new friendships when the only thoughts in my mind were of the utter devastation I was experiencing? Who wants to make friends with that?

I still don't know how I made it through. Jesus. It had to be Jesus. Because he was certainly there and gave me hope and comfort when there was nothing else to supply it. He gave promises of complete redemption and hope for the future, and he reminded me it would all work for my good. Still, there were days I stayed in bed. All day. While my kids played somewhere, doing something—I don't even know what. There were so many Netflix shows and a lot of ice cream and maybe a good deal of retail therapy. The latter felt somewhat justified—I had to replace a complete wardrobe, after all. I can't tell you of the days and weeks and months of depression where it felt like someone had socked me in the stomach and I could never function again. I still—even with Jesus—don't know how I made it through that. My heart broke completely, and I will never be the same again. You don't just get over something that takes the life you knew, shakes it up until it breaks, and then lets the pieces scatter.

I will never be the person that I was. Some fragile innocence and easy trust is gone. I can't get back my faith in humanity or in loved ones who were deceived. I don't understand God very well even though I used to think I did. I don't jive well with black-and-white statements or extreme paradigms anymore. Pain really hurts me—it always has—and I fear something like this happening again. Jesus helps, but I still battle hugely in my mind as I wait for him to redeem different areas. Sometimes the emotional and spiritual distance from my family weighs on me and, for a while, I'm just not so sure that God is good, because it really hurts.

No one "lives happily ever after" in a story like mine. There is a lot of hard mixed in with the good. Still, so much good has happened—in my heart as I saw God's all-compassionate love for me, and in my life as I have experienced the real transformation that comes with knowing and loving him. I could never go back. I would never want to.

—*Naomi R.*

I don't know where you are right now, if you're drowning or surviving, if you're watching your dreams flatline on the table or if they've been cold in the morgue for a while. You didn't choose it. This wasn't the plan.

slides plate of bacon toward you
pours cup of coffee
strokes your hair

I'm sorry.

Steering into the Surprise

Clint Barton: The city is flying and we're fighting an army of robots. And I have a bow and arrow. None of this makes sense.
—*Avengers: Age of Ultron*[1]

It might feel like the unfairness will never not chafe. It will always be right there digging into your ribs like the underwire on an old bra that's seen better days. I get that. Let's keep going anyway, okay? Like maybe what if it chafed, but you figured out how to hold the pain so that you could carry it a bit without tiring. Maybe use your imagination or pretend to look at it from someone else's point of view. Suspend your reality for a sec. Let's dare to peek around the corner at what could be someday, in a parallel dimension.

Sometimes, even if your circumstances get better, you still wrestle with the hurt of the earlier stuff. Just because you're in a good place now doesn't mean all the hurt feelings magically evaporate. In my daughter Ana's case, no matter how fair we try to make things now, we can't make up for the nine years of unfairness. When she laments it's not fair about a piece of candy, I know that underlying the present situation is a lifetime that we can never redo. All we can do is move forward together.

After all the infertility and complications with the pregnancy, I was so grateful for my son, but if I was really honest, even though God had finally answered my prayers, I still wasn't content. And I struggled with guilt for wanting more. Maybe you've had these kinds of thoughts:

God, I know I finally have a baby, but now I want another one, okay?

I know I finally have a job, but I want to advance in my field, and a raise would be super.

Thanks for the clear report after chemo, but now take away that feeling of looking over my shoulder for the other shoe to drop.

When It Isn't Enough

What do you do when you get everything you asked for and it isn't enough? When you hope and pray and dream and cry out and then you get your answer and it's yes, you're supposed to feel grateful, right? Have you ever gotten your yes, only to discover that it wasn't enough? That you're still incomplete? And then you feel guilty and try to make yourself experience the gratitude you know you should feel. And when you can't conjure up enough thankfulness and you still feel a hole in your heart, you shove more guilt in the hole to try to force yourself to accept your life.

After I finally had my child and the title of Mommy and was spending my days with diapers and playdates, I felt extremely thankful. I thanked God for the gift of answered prayer.

> **Via Twitter @UnexpectedMel**
>
> *Elliott: Mommy, does my hair look okay? Did I brush it okay?*
>
> *Me: It looks beautiful . . . I mean handsome. You look amazing. I'm in love.*
>
> *Elliott: Well, you're already married.*

But as time wore on and our final round of in vitro came and went unsuccessfully, I began to feel those old feelings of anguish and longing creep back up and grow tentacles into my heart. Dang it. Why couldn't I just be grateful, and what was wrong with me that I had the gall to tell God it wasn't enough?

"Enough" finally came to me in an unusual way.

Growing up in northeastern Ohio, I learned how to drive in a blizzard. Snow and ice were the norm, and one of the first things I learned about driving was if your car spun out in a turn, you should steer into the skid. As my life has taken unexpected turns and skids, I've adopted the same strategy—steering into the surprise.

After my dream of more babies in my belly died and I skidded out, I gingerly wrapped my fingers around the wheel and turned into the skid. The dream was dead. But maybe there was something else . . . or different . . . or better on the other side.

Via Twitter @UnexpectedMel

Evie: Mama? We should definitely not swallow other people's throw up, right?

Me: I am so scared.

And Then

I thought it was over. Grand adventures were for twenty-year-olds on summer break, and I had a husband and child, and I settled into big-time hunkering in the land of golf carts and capri pants.

And then the unexpected. God woke me up from my cushy suburban stupor and set my heart on fire for the rest of the world, his people in poverty, the ones outside of the bubble. Orphans and widows . . . so many mentions in the Bible. I read with new eyes. Had they always been in there? How had I missed it?

God nudged me, and I said yes. Yes. Such a short, simple word that led me down the rabbit hole of faith into a life of purpose, a world in need. The minivan mama with a calling, now I'm the one having the grand adventures.

Unexpected joy. Unexpected friendships. Unexpected lessons. I'm on the God-ride. And you can be too. All you have to do is say yes.

We often meet the unexpected. What if instead of freaking out, turning away, *running* away, we freaking turn *toward*, run *to* the unexpected? What if we *steer into the surprise?*

Via Unexpected.org

On Hunkering

11/1/2009

After our long struggle to have Elliott, move to the 'burbs, start our own company, and fix up our house, it would be tempting to hunker down. To enjoy the fruits of our labor and, above all, keep it safe. But I don't want to be a hunkerer. I'm pretty sure that's not what God intended for any of us to do.

Every day I hold out my hands to God and open them, palms up. "God, it's yours. My life, my son, my marriage, our adoption process, our stuff . . . yours." And so if everything is God's, then what does he want me to do with it? Do I hoard it or do I share it? We are blessed with so much love in our house. I want to take it out, share it, add to it. I don't want to get so wrapped up in staying safe that I fail to see what's outside of my little realm. I don't want to be a hunkerer.

When I give up hunkering, life gets really exciting. Where will God take me next? I can't wait to find out where he's going to take me and what he'll have me do. Following God truly is the most exciting adventure I've ever had. The first step is opening my hands and releasing my white-knuckled grip on my life.

God, don't let me hunker. Save me from my own notion of safety, and let me feel safe in your arms, not in my stuff. I hold your blessings with open hands and acknowledge that you are Lord of my children, of my marriage, of my home, and of my life. Take me on an epic adventure and use the little bit of love in my heart to do mighty things for your world.

The Unexpected

I have always loved stories, devouring tales of bravery and vanquishing evil. I am a story-reader, a story-maker, and a storyteller. My soul sparkles with the words of changed lives and mended hearts and journeys lived for the glory of the Creator and Author of all.

Certain stories, though, kind of freak me out. I used to freak out a little when someone would tell a story of the miraculous. You know what I mean. The kind where somebody miraculously stood up and walked, like within our lifetime and not back in the Bible. The kind of encounters with God that are supernatural and unexplainable. I had a hard time believing any of that. Until something weird happened to me.

After praying for God to heal my body for years and years, one day I discovered that he'd answered my prayers. Only in his unexpected God-way. I woke up one morning to discover that he'd healed my heart.

For a few months after counseling, I experienced peace about having one child and being done with family building. I was filled with acceptance and thankfulness, and all the struggley feelings of the last few years had ebbed away, replaced with a newfound contentment. I liked my life. Briefly.

And then, feelings that we weren't complete, that there was more, began creeping back in. That old desire for a big family returned (Darn you, *7th Heaven!*), and I couldn't shake it or make it go away. I started to wonder about in vitro again, but my allergic reactions to the drugs kept getting worse the more I took, and I worried that my body couldn't take another round without something serious happening.

In all the years I'd prayed for healing, I figured if miracles were real, then God would make me fertile, that my body would, *Poof!*, start making babies. I never, ever considered that God could heal my broken heart. But one morning, I woke up, and the incapacitating heart pain, all the longing for a baby in my belly, was better.

And that was six years ago. Somehow overnight, God had healed my heart. Kinda freaky and weird. But wait, there's more.

The night before, my mom had awakened in the middle of the night, gripped with fear for me that I'd hurt myself doing more fertility needles and drugs, and started praying. The next day, I woke up with acceptance of my infertility and a passion for adoption.

Steering. Into. The surprise.

I Never Saw This Coming

Adoption? Are you kidding me? I never saw this coming. (I wish I could tell you that I've always "had a heart for" adoption and Africa like so many other Christians, but that would be lying. I "had a heart for" new hardwood flooring and Pottery Barn bedspreads. Which are awesome.) That day, I had a conversation with God about Africa. After learning about the guinea worms in science class in seventh grade, I told God I would NEVER, ever go to Africa. Every time the freaky missions people at church talked about Africa, Alex and I would whisper to each other, "Isn't there somewhere else to go?" Jonah (swallowed by a fish Jonah) didn't want to go to the city of Nineveh, and I was taking it one step further. I would avoid an entire continent. I was convinced if I stepped foot on African soil, I'd immediately have guinea worms springing from my eyeballs.

(I didn't know. My ignorance is appalling.)

One thing I've figured out over the years is that God loves it when we use the word NEVER. When we say we'll never do something, it's like he flags it on his supernatural ECHELON system. "Oops, they said 'never.' Taking probability of event happening to 100 percent. Bahahahaha! They're gonna love this."

Here are a few *nevers* we've said over the years: "I'll never have kids," "We'll never go to Africa," "We'll never adopt out of birth order." Just whatever. God thinks he's hilarious.

We watched a video at church about the kids living on the streets in Nairobi, Kenya, and that day I told God, Maayyybe I would go on a mission trip. He nudged me. Okay, maybe the next time the children's choir visits, we could host some of the kids, you know, since we have this big house with extra room for all the kids we can't have. He nudged me harder. Okay, I'll adopt. Yay, I'll adopt!

Wait, what? In one day, I went from devastating sadness about infertility to healed heart and an excitement to adopt, as if I'd invented adoption and it was my idea all along. In. One. Day.

That night, after my epiphany about adoption, Alex, Elliott, and I went to Ted's Montana Grill for some eco-friendly bison, and I mentioned to Alex that I'd been thinking that we should start the adoption process. I'd only just gotten to this place, like, a minute ago, so I figured Alex was nowhere near it.

He always surprises me. He said something like, "It just doesn't feel like"—and I mentally finished his sentence, "it's the right thing for us" or "we need another child because Elliott is enough"—and instead I heard, "our family is complete. I've been thinking about adoption too." What? Really? Unbeknownst to me, Alex had been hired to work on adoption-related design projects and had spent weeks staring at photos of orphaned children. My insides started to smile.

In talking to family members, I discovered that a bunch of them had been praying for a long time for us to develop a desire to adopt. Apparently they all cosmically ganged up on us and we never saw it coming. And I'm so glad they did. I probably owe all of them a fruit basket or something.

I think of this as my Damascus Road experience. (Let's see, I've compared myself to Jonah and the Big Fish and now the apostle Paul and the Damascus Road Conversion. Stop me if I try to add in Daniel and the Lion's Den.) It was like scales fell from my eyes, and I realized that my infertility wasn't the end. It was the beginning.

We steered into the surprise. Adoption. Africa. Ethiopia. And it felt really, really right.

(Note of irony: After all those years of being scared of a

mission trip to Africa, I figured I'd go kicking and screaming. When I finally took my first trip to Uganda with HopeChest and the plane touched down on the runway in Entebbe, I sobbed tears of joy. Uganda's now my favorite place on earth. I'm completely obsessed with the entire gorgeous continent and all the people on it, and I was wrong and a big idiot. God has a fantastic sense of humor. And he's really smart.)

(Note of caution: Apparently God uses the least likely people in the world to do unexpected things. That way he gets all the credit because no one would ever believe we could come up with this stuff on our own. You've been warned, fellow idiots.)

I Get to Do This

I began to see my infertility, this noose choking me for over a decade, as a conduit into this unexplored world of adoption. Lots of people adopt without being infertile, but for me, the infertility is what walked me up to the front stoop, rang the doorbell, and introduced me to adoption when it answered the door.

After I started the adoption process, several people unexpectedly laid hands on my womb and prayed for healing and I silently prayer-blocked them. "No-no, God, no, you've healed my heart. Please leave my uterus alone. I'm good." I no longer wanted pregnancy. I wanted adoption. (Couple things here. One, maybe don't put your hands on someone's general womb region in the middle of prayer unless you know them really, really well and even then, nah. Two, prayer-blocking is a thing. Maybe not a real thing, but a girl can try.)

My whole mind-set shifted. I kept thinking, "I get to do this." I was giddy about providing a home for a child who needed a family, and I was excited to never, ever try to make a baby again. And I felt this spiritual connection to another mother somewhere in Ethiopia. I prayed for her every day, like we were in partnership and somehow through prayer I could serve her as a spiritual midwife, tending to her across the miles.

Via Unexpected.org
10/21/2009

My dear sweet baby,

You are in your birth mother's belly right now, but you are in my heart. I pray for you every day, for you and for the precious woman carrying you inside of her. I pray that both of you would feel loved and supported, protected, and nourished. I pray that God would hug you both for me. Oh, my sweet baby, I can't wait to hug you myself, to snuggle with you, and laugh with you, and nuzzle noses. I catch myself thinking of you throughout the day, and my insides fill with joy at the thought of you. You are precious to me.

Love,
Mommy

With adoption, I gained new context for the ultimate unfairness. A mother losing her child. A child losing a mother. So much loss.

This is sacred work. When you move into adoption, you're standing on holy ground. To humble yourself and enter into a child's pain, to hold the loss, to tuck up the brokenness into your family and say, "We will carry this together." I began to look beyond my own unfairness of infertility into the unfairness of a child who's lost the one thing she should be entitled to—a family.

Via Twitter @UnexpectedMel
The girls are playing dolls, pretending to run an orphanage for dolls without parents. #adoption #orphancare

And so. I've steered into the surprise and experienced the highest highs and the lowest lows. The life I have now is so unexpected, so different from the adorable little paper doll world of my imagination. Within the mystery of this newfound life, rising like a phoenix out of the ashes, I've found the one thing I never thought to look for. Joy.

The Excruciating Pain of Joy

Angel: You can be a rainbow and not a pain-bow.

—Angel[1]

People always talk about the difference between joy and happiness. I've decided the big difference is that joy hurts. Happiness is a wonderful feeling and joy is a daily dying to your original plans and scooping up God's plans and not hating him for them. I love happiness. Happiness is the feeling I get when I open up a new Nerds Rope. Joy is deeper, and it is painful.

In *Shattered Dreams*, Larry Crabb says,

> Our shattered dreams are never random. They are always a piece in a larger puzzle, a chapter in a larger story. Pain is a tragedy. But it's never only a tragedy. For the Christian, it's always a necessary mile on the long journey to joy.[2]

I don't hold babies. For one thing, I'm extremely clumsy and worry I'll somehow trip while standing still and fling the child through the air while we all watch in horrified slow motion. And also, holding babies releases inside me this painful well of emotion, and I cannot bear it in my every day, walking down the street trying not to ugly cry in public, life. (Note to self: Get more counseling.) Every time I see a mother with her newborn baby, with all the love and health between them, without the brokenness of orphanhood and loss and attachment struggles and needles and hospitals and diagnoses, I die to my original plan, lay it down, and hug tighter this twisting, sometimes writhing path of beauty in the pain. Crabb again:

The richest hope permits the deepest suffering, which releases the strongest power, which then produces the greatest joy . . . maybe there is no shortcut to joy.[3]

God's plan for my life involves a deeper joy than I could have ever imagined because it comes from a deeper pain than I thought possible. Joy hurts. It's part of that upside-down kingdom that Jesus was talking about in Matthew 5: "Blessed are those who mourn" (v. 4).

We want all of the blessings without any of the mourning. But as I've laid my original dreams in their coffin and lowered it into the ground, mourned the death, and felt the fullness of the loss, I've felt joy pricking up through the surface of my soul, searing my skin, resurrecting me for new dreams, new life, new purpose. Those who mourn are blessed. That's really whacked . . . and oddly true. Joy filling your sad heart to the brim hurts, aches, like stretching wineskins. Your shriveled heart feels like it will burst right open when it starts to beat again.

Jessica's Story Continued: My Son with Autism Is One of the Greatest Gifts

I didn't know what to do, so I prayed. I begged, "God, please, teach me how to be a mother worthy of this boy. Teach me how to be thankful. Teach me how to have joy. I need your peace. Please help me." I choked out words through hysterical tears, and pulled myself together, and rejoined my family. Still shaken and defeated.

I have never had a prayer answered more directly in my entire life. The next week, I shared my struggle with my small group. The things I was telling myself, the way I felt. They prayed too. Within a week, it was like a switch flipped. God showed me a new thing—he showed me that joy was a choice, and it was one that I could make. I choose to believe that God is in control. I choose to believe that this boy is one of the greatest gifts given to me. I choose to believe that there is more to life than being like everyone else. I choose to believe that Jesus is all that matters. I choose joy.

Now, I feel a freedom that I have never felt before, I feel like I am able to relish and immerse myself in the parenting of Knox and actually enjoy it. Because I don't have to do life like everyone else does. I know at the core of my soul that God makes beauty out of my mess. That, according to Romans 8:28: "And we know that in all things God works for the good of those who love him, who have been called according to his purpose." I truly believe that God doesn't make bad things happen. The bad in this life is a result of sin run rampant in a fallen world. BUT. He can take the most stressful, scary, crazy things and turn them into something wonderful. He can take a little boy's autism and use it to show his mother that she is not bound by this world's definition of good or right or perfect. Because Knox's worth (and mine) is found in the eyes of Jesus Christ.

—Jessica W.

God Sewed Africa into My Heart

When God ripped my heart apart, I had to paint a picture to process all my feelings. He ripped it apart, destroyed my hopes of squatting natural births to push babies into the world, then sewed in Africa and orphan care and adoption. Each rip and each stitch stung. And when he was through, my heart was bigger. He increased its capacity by however big I was willing to trust him and follow. The new life force rushing through it overwhelmed me.

I painted my heart blackish purplish red, and I painted the continent of Africa inside bright and orange and vibrant, pushing at the limits of my heart. I trickled gray tears down the heart. And then I took staples and needle and thread and sewed Africa into my heart. I decoupaged words and Bible verses all around. I didn't sleep until the painting was done. It was my way of capturing or commemorating the change. I jabbed the needle and thread into the canvas over and over. I felt the prick on my finger.

Joy hurts. Heart surgery is excruciating. The recovery takes time. But those who mourn are blessed.

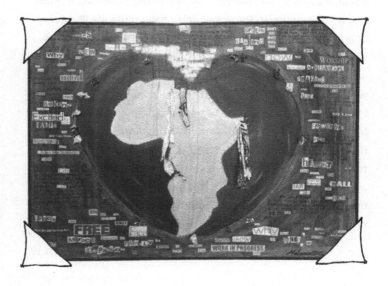

Via guest post at EverydaysBest.com
February 15, 2012

Perhaps the most boggling thing that I have learned about waiting is the intense JOY that it brings. I don't mean the exhale at the end of the wait. I mean that I have come to the mind-blowing realization that joy is feeling emotionally broken and bloody, and sitting with Jesus, who knows a little something about brokenness. Sitting in the Father's lap, exhausted from the battle, but feeling so close SO CLOSE to him, hearing his voice so near. Joy in the pain of the wait.[4]

Where Do We Go from Here?

Flight Attendant Steve: You have three seconds to get back to your seat.

Annie: No one can get anywhere in three seconds. You're setting me up for a loss already.

—*Bridesmaids*[1]

Dear Ana, Elliott, and Evie,

I love you guys so much. I still can't believe I have children shrieking up and down our halls. I'm a barren woman living in a fertile house. My womb is closed but our doors are open.

Ana, I'm so sorry for everything that led up to you needing us in the first place. I'm sorry you have to miss home even as you learn to love this new one. You are brave and compassionate and so gifted at making friends. You are the most adaptable person I know. Your energy keeps us all going.

Elliott, you've grown into a creative, clever boy, and even though my body tried to kill you, you've risen above the preemie complications and are thriving against all odds. You're our little miracle, the boy who lived. Your laugh is my favorite music and your imagination knows no bounds.

Evie, I'm so sorry for all your question marks, for losses you can't even fully identify. The life you should've had blurs like a fading dream on the edges of your conscious mind, and I see you squinting for understanding. You are bold and strong and brilliant and no one, I mean no one, puts baby in a corner.

Our family is forged out of brokenness. Our infertility,

Elliott's difficult birth, Evie's and Ana's huge losses of first families and cultures. Kids, even our new dog, JPEG, was bound with wire and left by a dumpster to die. Talk about unfair.

And yet. God helped us find each other for healing, for loving, and every day we make something beautiful out of the ashes. I am so grateful for my whole family.

I love our life together.

Love, Mom

My whole family is together because of unfairness. It's a weird thing, wishing with all my heart the unfair stuff hadn't happened to any of us while simultaneously being incredibly grateful that we're all together because of it. Infertility, loss, sickness, autism, mental illness, death, countless transitions, and layers of pain. We didn't choose any of it. But we've learned to love it. And we learn to love it more every day.

Sometimes I have to blink to see if this is real. My life. I whisper to myself, "I get to do this." This life I never saw coming, not in a million years of planning. Our family is raw and real and layered. Each week there is fresh pain, a new unfairness, but we are learning together. I love my extraordinary kids so much I feel like I can't breathe typing this. And I could've missed it. I could've missed *them*. If I had gotten precisely what I thought I wanted a million years ago.

The God Ride

Picture yourself getting on a roller coaster. Part of the ride is waiting in line for a crazy long time. You're sunburned and annoyed and the person behind you smells like the bottom of a garbage can. Sometimes it feels like the line will never move, but you watch the coaster loop around up ahead and know that it'll be worth it if you just wait.

When it's finally your turn, finally, after all that waiting, you step into your little coaster car and ease into your seat. You fasten your seat belt, and that harness thingy comes down over your shoulders. You've waited all this time, and now you're feeling a little nervous. Maybe this wasn't such a good idea. Just as you think about running away, the ride takes off and you're inching up a really steep hill. During the climb, you have nowhere to go and the terror crawls into your throat and you hear the car *clack clack clacking* to the top. The climb feels like forever.

You finally make it to the top and feel like you're going to barf. The car starts down, and for a moment you hang over the top until you plunge down, loop, and spin. The wind punches your face and your lips blow open into a grinning scream. Your stomach feels like it's dangling out the back of the car. After plummeting to new lows and rising to new heights and spinning till you can't spin anymore, you land back at the beginning with bugs in your teeth and a smile askew on your windblown face. It was terrible. And wonderful.

This is what I call the God-ride. It's waiting endlessly, feeling petrified, fighting vomit, miles of anticipation, and whirling, racing, plunging through the air. It's exhilarating, and you want to go again and again.

I didn't choose this unexpected God-ride, but I love it with all my ripped-apart, sewn-back-together heart. I'm so glad for every moment of the journey, even the moments when I thought I wouldn't make it, because now I get it. Now I understand. All the pain. All the waiting. It was all for them. I'm not the same person I was when I started. I'm still in progress. I'm still a mess. But I'm their mess. I'm their mom. And it took the whole journey to bring me here.

I want us to walk into a life of thankfulness and security in God's grace. Our circumstances may not change, but as we walk together, we can experience joy. It's not fair. It's absolutely not fair. It's hair-raising and occasionally stomach-churning. And it's oh so exhilarating.

Scars Can Be Beautiful

I've been changed by a God who loved me through disappointment and continues to carry me through the unfairness of life. I've discovered, through personal struggle and partnering to alleviate the struggles of others, the intense joy that comes through the pain, through unfairness. I've moved from desperation and desolation into gratitude and grace. Rather than listing all the ways life isn't fair, I begin to offer praise, and in the praising, I worship deeper, love harder, and experience God's pleasure.

I just reread that last paragraph and am equal parts mm-hmming and wanting to gag myself with the nearest available spatula. It's all true . . . half of the time. The other half I'm still a big whiner. It's a work in progress, blah blah something about the journey blah.

After years of telling God it's not fair, I can now say that I'm grateful for my struggle. I would never, ever tell someone else to be grateful for theirs. We can't tell people in their pain to be grateful. That would be the highest cruelty. But over time, after having raw conversations with God and acknowledging the life unfolding around me, I see the beauty of his creation. It's not fair. It's different than fair. It's new and unique and it's mine.

Via Unexpected.org
January 28, 2013

I have a smiley face of scars on my belly. Two eyes, one over each ovary, a nose in my belly button, and a smile over and through my uterus. The eyes and nose came from laparoscopic surgery for the endometriosis, and my uterus got its smile when they rescued my in vitro miracle boy from my protesting womb.

I was self-conscious. The smile was so bumpy for the first few years that you could see it through my bathing suit. After years of trying to get pregnant and then months of "planning" a natural birth, I pictured the word FAILURE scrawled across the scar in jagged black Sharpie.

After years of anorexia segued into years of infertility segued into the beginnings of fine lines and screaming joints, I've learned an important lesson. Our scars make us who we are. Our bumps and lumps aren't failures. They're stories. Scars represent healed wounds. Healed.

How spectacular that our God created us to heal. When little ones trip over too-big shoes and rip gashes through baby-soft flesh, we apply boo-boo juice and a robot Band-Aid and they heal. Each day, the skin sews itself back together. Or a needle sews it back together. Rips heal, scars fade, and giggles return. We were made to heal.

I have some heart-wounds right now. Do you? I stare at my smiley-faced belly and I am reminded that I was created to heal. Not just from physical wounds, but from heart-wounds too. The boo-boos on my soul need attention. I offer them to the Healer.

When I was a child, we used to gather at my grandparents' house with the whole family for Christmas. On Christmas morning, we'd tear into presents, and there would be these little gifts without bows tucked in with everything else. My aunt loved estate-sale shopping, and throughout the year she'd find little surprises that made her think of us and she'd scoop them up and save them. These weren't the expected gifts, the ones with the shiny bows front and center under the Christmas tree. These were the unexpected bonus gifts, unadorned and tucked amongst the fancier things. She called them "no-bows."

For months, I've been wondering how to end this book. I kept writing paragraphs with happy words about how we'll all be okay and this is better and everything is fine. But then last night, as I scrunched my head into my pillow after screaming myself hoarse at my kids' swim meet, I realized what I needed to write, and it's a little terrifying.

There is no neat little bow on top. Nothing can quite tie it all together. This unexpected life is a no-bow.

I was falling for the very thing I've criticized inside these pages, this need we have to find the right platitude that will make it all better. I was platituding myself. But there is no bow. Whatever you're going through right now or whatever you've been through, it's hard, maybe it's awful, and it will leave a mark. There will be times when you stare at a wall, and times when you wave your fist in the air, and times when you'll feel like you're tearing apart. And there will be scars. And there will always be those things people say or photos you see that will take you right back to that feeling of helplessness or desperation. There will be triggers. You are marked.

There is no bow. But what I've learned and what I've seen in my own life and in the lives of so many other brave warriors is that we do learn to love our lives, as is, with the scars, naked and bowless. Scars can be beautiful.

So to end this time together, I won't say everything will be okay. How could I know that? I'll just look you in the eye, give you a nod of solidarity, and smile.

There, peeping among the cloud-wrack above a dark tower high up in the mountains, Sam saw a white star twinkle for a while. The beauty of it smote his heart, as he looked up out of the forsaken land, and hope returned to him. For like a shaft, clear and cold, the thought pierced him that in the end the Shadow was only a small and passing thing: there was light and high beauty for ever beyond its reach.

J. R. R. Tolkien, *The Return of the King*[2]

Acknowledgments

Elliott, you came first and made me a mommy. Thanks for your complete trust to give your floppy little preemie body into the hands of such a newbie. I'm sorry I tried to feed you whole Chick-fil-A nuggets when you were nine months old. I didn't know and you're okay, so let's not squabble over how I could've done it differently. I love laughing with you and staying up late to talk *Harry Potter* and horcruxes.

Evie, you burst into my life, and the sheer force of your ginormous personality turned everything Technicolor. You have so much to say, and thanks for teaching me to listen. You're extraordinary, and I can't wait to see everything that you do, because I'm pretty sure you're going to take over the world. Your little hand in mine has taught me so much.

Ana Banana, you are pure light. Your laughter fills the house and you care about people so deeply. I lurrve our talks together and how you can eat bacon three meals a day. Thanks for your patience with me as you and I figure out how to skip a whole childhood and pick up in the tween years. I feel like neither one of us knows exactly what we're doing, but we're in this together. I'm your biggest fan.

Kathy Helmers, you're the bestest. This book wouldn't be a book without you. You helped pull the theme out of my ramblings on "it's not fair" and your subtitle "Learning to Love the Life You Didn't Choose" became my guidepost for the whole thing. Thanks for saving my readers from a bajillion trite sayings about "life's a journey." Your BS detector is on point. Your front porch is one of my happy places, with its twinkle lights, Balvenie, and The Bruce's doggy head for patting.

Sandy Vander Zicht, the entire time I was writing this and

feeling totally adrift, I kept telling myself that if I could just get the words out, you could fix it. Just get it to Sandy. Thanks again for taking a chance on a new, weird writer.

Lori Vanden Bosch, thank you for bringing order to all these words. I felt a bit like I bled out onto a Word document, and then you came in and moved everything into place like a Rubik's Cube mad genius. Whovians unite.

Alicia Kasen and Jennifer VerHage, I still can't believe I get to work with you guys. You are ridiculously fun people and so good at what you do. Nancy Erickson, thank you for your impeccable eye for detail and for knowing the difference between awhile and a while. I never will. Tom Dean, Joyce Ondersma, and the rest of the Zonderpeeps, air kisses and gratitude.

Readers of Unexpected.org. Thanks for your online friendship. It's a distinct privilege to write for you. You make me a better writer. Thanks for showing me what matters to you and for helping me feel not alone when I put myself out there. I'm convinced you're the most gracious and fun people on the Internet. I'm grateful.

To my HopeChest friends, the ones in the States and the ones in Uganda and Guatemala, thanks for teaching me how to love well and showing me that hope is tangible. Joseph, I can't wait to eat another fish eyeball with you.

Adult adoptees and those who grew up in foster care. To my friends in real life and the ones I read on the Internet, I'm so grateful for your voices. You're teaching me so much about how to parent my girls, how to respect them, their birth cultures, and their families of origin. I know I don't always get it right, but I continue to listen and learn from you. Please keep speaking and writing the hard truth.

To the women who've shared their stories within these pages, thank you thank you thank you. I'm in awe of you. I'm humbled by your life experience and wisdom. Thank you for sharing it with me. You make this book rounder, deeper. I only hope my words are worthy to share these pages with yours.

Mom, thanks for all the "poor babies" and for modeling so well what it is to learn to love a life you didn't choose. You are a brainy blonde warrior, and it's an honor to carry your crazy laugh into the next generation. Daddy, thanks for holding the tissue box while I cried, for all the cups of coffee and conversation we've had over the years, and for showing me what it looks like to follow Jesus.

Chantel, I just absolutely love you times infinity. Thank you for reading my draft before I turned it in. Your encouraging words kept me going when I felt like this was impossible.

Ashlee and my fellow *Coffee+Crumbs* writers, I love and respect our tribe so much. Courtney, Jeannie, and Allison, thanks for taking my calls and walking me through the last year. Courtney, we're gonna need another sleepover soon.

Alex. I have no idea what to say to you. How do I thank my best friend for nights like this while I was finishing my manuscript:

You: I went ahead and made mac and cheese and a frozen
    pizza for the kids.
Me: Is it dinnertime?
You: Yeah. I got it. It's okay.
Me: What day is it?
You: Wednesday.
Me: I haven't showered since Sunday.
You: I know.

I'm so glad you're always brutally honest with me about my writing. You make me better and I love you like crazy. All we really want to do is drink Coke slushies and sit on the couch bingeing *Agents of SHIELD*, but we keep having these adventures. Thank you for steering into the surprises with me.

God, thanks for never leaving or forsaking me. And thanks for the freedom to worship you in limbo. I'm really glad you're so big I can't figure you out. It's actually comforting.

Getting involved with HopeChest has changed my life. I've witnessed the community with which we partner move from living in a government camp waiting for handouts to developing income-generating projects, educational opportunities, and doing leadership and vocational development. I'm in total awe watching it all unfold and feel like I have a front-row seat to God's beating heart. HopeChest works in Russia, Swaziland, Ethiopia, Uganda, Moldova, India, Guatemala, and the US. If you're interested in hearing about how your church, group of friends, or community can get involved, I'd be completely humbled and honored to tell you more. Email me at unexpectedmel@unexpected.org or visit hopechest.org.

My friends Chantel and Ginny started a doll company called Forever We that teaches kids how to be compassionate friends. Their first doll, Jewel, helps raise money for childhood cancer research and comes with a port in her chest and a removable wig, a courage bead, a dress, and a hospital gown, as well as a book about two young friends and what happens when one of them has cancer. They also have a superhero doll with a little mask and cape. You will explode with cuteness overload. You can even sponsor an entire hospital so that all the kids with cancer get dolls. I know. My friends are amazing. Check them out at foreverwe.org.

Notes

Chapter 1: A Help-Each Other Book
1. *The Princess Bride*, directed by Rob Reiner, Act III Communications, 1987.
2. Madeleine L'Engle, *A Wrinkle in Time* (New York: Farrar Straus Giroux, 1962), 69.

Chapter 2: I Feel Your Pain
1. *Anchorman*, directed by Adam McKay, DreamWorks, 2004.

Chapter 3: The Heart Cry of the Entire Human Race
1. *Labyrinth*, directed by Jim Henson, Henson Associates, 1986.

Chapter 4: How to Fall Apart Like a Boss
1. *The Wedding Singer*, directed by Frank Coraci, New Line Cinema, 1998.

Chapter 5: Digging Out from a Good Wallow
1. *Galaxy Quest*, directed by Dean Parisot, DreamWorks SKG, 1999.

Chapter 6: Complaint as a Spiritual Discipline
1. *Superstar*, directed by Bruce McCulloch, SNL Studios, 1999.
2. Ann Voskamp, *One Thousand Gifts* (Grand Rapids: Zondervan, 2010), 149.

Chapter 7: So Totes Righteously Angry on Your Behalf
1. *Tommy Boy*, directed by Peter Segal, Paramount Pictures, 1995.

Chapter 8: Fighting Emotional Gangrene

1. "Prophecy Girl," *Buffy the Vampire Slayer*, WB Television Network, aired June 2, 1997.

Chapter 9: Comfort Foods That Will Help You Eat Your Feelings

1. *Better Off Dead*, directed by Savage Steve Holland, A & M Films, 1985.
2. Kate Merker, *Real Simple*, www.realsimple.com/food-recipes/browse-all-recipes/gnocchi-sausage-spinach.

Chapter 10: Because Sometimes Suffering Is Funny

1. *Waiting for Guffman*, directed by Christopher Guest, Castle Rock Entertainment, 1996.
2. J. K. Rowling, *Harry Potter and the Prisoner of Azkaban* (New York: Scholastic, 1999).
3. *Elizabethtown*, directed by Cameron Crowe, Paramount Pictures, 2005.
4. *Austin Powers: International Man of Mystery*, directed by Jay Roach, New Line Cinema, 1997.

Chapter 11: Don't Make Me Come Over There

1. "Consumed," *The Walking Dead*, American Movie Classics, aired November 16, 2014.

Chapter 12: Living Like a Cadbury Egg

1. *Monty Python and the Holy Grail*, directed by Terry Gilliam and Terry Jones, Michael White Productions, 1975.

Chapter 13: Count the Wins (Even While You're Losing)

1. *Pitch Perfect*, directed by Jason Moore, Gold Circle Films, 2012.
2. *Just Married*, directed by Shawn Levy, Twentieth Century Fox, 2003.

Chapter 14: Things You Should Say If You Want a Good Face Punch

1. *Elf*, directed by Jon Favreau, New Line Cinema, 2003.

2. *Happy Gilmore*, directed by Dennis Dugan, Universal Pictures, 1996.

Chapter 15: Faking Healthy and the I'm Fine Smile

1. "Once More, with Feeling," *Buffy the Vampire Slayer*, WB Television Network, aired November 6, 2001.

Chapter 16: Awkward Hugging

1. "The Magician's Apprentice," *Doctor Who*, British Broadcasting Company, aired September 19, 2015.

Chapter 17: The Two Most Powerful Words

1. "Secrets and Lies," *30 Rock*, NBC Studios, aired December 6, 2007.
2. *Austin Powers: The Spy Who Shagged Me*, directed by Jay Roach, New Line Cinema, 1999.

Chapter 18: 100 Things You Can Do to Help

1. *Couples Retreat*, directed by Peter Billingsley, Universal Pictures, 2009.

Chapter 19: Her Cupcake Is Better Than Mine

1. *Willy Wonka & the Chocolate Factory*, directed by Mel Stuart, Wolper Pictures Ltd., 1971.
2. Philip Yancey, *Disappointment with God* (Grand Rapids: Zondervan, 1988), 67.
3. Ibid., 56.

Chapter 20: You Went to the Zoo

1. *Sky High*, directed by Mike Mitchell, Walt Disney Pictures, 2005.

Chapter 21: Why Do Bad Things Happen?

1. "Kill the Moon," *Doctor Who*, British Broadcasting Company, aired October 4, 2014.
2. Nadia Bolz-Weber, *Pastrix* (New York: Jericho, 2013), xvi.
3. Philip Yancey, *Where Is God When It Hurts?* (Grand Rapids: Zondervan, 1977, 1990), 229.

Chapter 22: Failure, Doubt, and Being Bananaballs

1. *Elizabethtown*, directed by Cameron Crowe, Paramount Pictures, 2005.
2. Preston Yancey, *Tables in the Wilderness* (Grand Rapids: Zondervan, 2014), 23.

Chapter 23: Everything Will Be Okay If . . .

1. *Space Camp*, directed by Harry Winer, ABC Motion Pictures, 1986.

Chapter 24: A Bunch of Bible Stuff for All Your Various Moods

1. "Jaynestown," *Firefly*, 20th Century Fox Television, aired October 18, 2002.
2. Christine Caine, *Undaunted* (Grand Rapids: Zondervan, 2012), 55.

Chapter 25: How to Survive the Death of a Dream

1. *Just Friends*, directed by Roger Kumble, New Line Cinema, 2005.

Chapter 26: Steering into the Surprise

1. *Avengers: Age of Ultron*, directed by Joss Whedon, Marvel Studios, 2015.

Chapter 27: The Excruciating Pain of Joy

1. "Sense and Sensitivity," *Angel*, WB Television Network, aired November 9, 1999.
2. Larry Crabb, *Shattered Dreams* (Colorado Springs: WaterBrook, 2001), 4.
3. Ibid., 42.
4. Melanie Dale, "On Waiting and God's Timing," www.every daysbest.com/2012/02/on-waiting-and-gods-timing.html.

Chapter 28: Where Do We Go from Here?

1. *Bridesmaids*, directed by Paul Feig, Universal Pictures, 2011.
2. J. R. R. Tolkien, *The Return of the King* (New York: Houghton Mifflin, 1955), 901.

Women are Scary

The Totally Awkward Adventure of Finding Mom Friends

Melanie Dale

Let's see...this is the part where I convince you that you need this book. This book will massage your feet. This book will bring you a fuzzy blanket at the end of a long day of parenting your tiny little insanazoids. I promise to make you snort laugh at least once. After reading this book, you'll rock jazz hands, be able to sing on-key, and never, ever have to fold laundry again.

Okay, they told me I'm actually supposed to tell you a little about the book. Um, right. Look. Here's the thing. Too many of us women are frazzled and lonely, isolated in our minivans while schlepping bags, strollers, and munchkins to and fro across town. It doesn't have to be this way.

In this guide to "momlationships," I use a dating analogy to take us "around the bases" to our home-run friendships, the ones that last a lifetime, not just a soccer season. This is our journey to each other, to finding our people and being other people's people, to learning how to bless each other and not destroy each other. It's sometimes scary. And always awkward. Let's have some fun.